Murder
by
Medicine

Murder
by
Medicine

A brilliant new
SleuthHound Mystery

B. F. Cayzer

SleuthHound Books
Atlanta, Lake Worth

SleuthHound Books

SleuthHound Books is an imprint of and published by Humanics Publishing Group, a division of Brumby Holdings, Inc. Its trademark, consisting of the words "SleuthHound Books" and portrayal of a bloodhound is registered in the U.S. Patent and Trademark Office and in other countries.

Brumby Holdings, Inc.
12 S. Dixie Hwy, Ste. 203
Lake Worth, FL 33460
USA

Printed in the United States of America and the United Kingdom

ISBN (Paperback) 0-89334-447-8
ISBN (Hardcover) 0-89334-446-X

Library of Congress Control Number: 2003310353

Dedicated to
Her Majesty Queen Elizabeth II

Table of Contents

This is a work of fiction. Names, characters, places and incidents are either the product of the author's imagination or used fictitiously. Happily, most of the places exist.

1

Being broke was awful. That's what I was thinking, seated at my desk in the tack room of Howe's Kentucky stables, waiting for the horses to come back from evening gallops and feeling anxious to go home to my darling Happy, aka Hillary. It was cold for October, and I put on a sweater.

My name is Rick Harrow. I'm British-born, but having been headhunted years ago to work in Florida before this job in Howe's stables, I'd got spoiled.

Spoiled for other things too.

Not that my Kentucky bride or I have ever been really rich. Happy, my wife, drew her best pay when she worked as a girl jockey.

As for me, the only time I came close to 'big money' was when I was still employed as an assistant trainer by derby winning trainer Burl Smithey, and our star horse, Arrow, had an offer in the millions to be syndicated as a stallion.

With Happy newly pregnant, we had looked forward to my cut of the commission for Arrow's breeding syndication, but Burl put an end to my contract. According to Burl, he fired me because I'd overstepped my bounds.

He seethed, "My assistants keep to the yard, their eyes on the horse flesh, and their mouths shut! You cost me an owner. Get out!"

Three jockeys in Saratoga had been murdered. All three of those jockeys were girls who rode the racing circuit with Happy. I hadn't been willing to take the risk that Happy might be the next victim, so I fingered Arrow's owner as the murderer. No way was I going to stay to fight Burl for my rightful share of the lucre and jeopardize my expanding family. By nightfall, we were heading for the hills of eastern Kentucky, Happy's 'home country.'

We ended up bunking with Happy's "Paw," as she called him, on his small farm about one hundred miles outside of Lexington. I'd always loved Happy's accent, filled with Kentucky drawls and twangs, but as soon as we arrived she dropped her city accent, and threw out the ya'lls and recons like wild fire. Her true "mountain" roots sprang up and right out of her mouth. As she headed for the barn where Paw was feeding the chickens, Happy yelled back to me, "Follow me, darlin'! Come in and say hello to Paw."

Paw greeted me with a huge hug and said, "How do, boy." You must have been driving for hours. Pull up a chair and sit a spell." Then he turned to Happy. "You're looking a mite peaked, Happy girl. Got some grandchildren on the way, do you now?" Happy beamed, stuck her stomach out very far, and Paw gave it a rub. "That there's a big doin'. I's mighty proud of ya!"

Not able to join in their colorful 'mountain-folk' conversation, I just smiled, besotted with my beautiful Happy, and wondered how my British accent would go over if I ever got in a word. Then, from the far end of the barn, I heard sounds that were music to my ears -- the neighing of horses and hooves kicking against their stalls. Suddenly, I felt right at home.

After a month of visiting with the 'kin folk,' and tearing up the bluegrass pastures riding bareback, Happy said, "Rick, darlin', you've got to have a look in the want ads. If we don't hightail it out of here pretty soon, Paw won't ever let us pick up and go. Worst even, I may plum forget how to talk like a city girl."

With that in mind, I rushed out to get a copy of the Daily Earth, which always had a good racing and classified section. There was an ad for an assistant trainer, placed by a minor trainer with stables in southeast Texas. What interested me most was his offer of accommodation, a car, as well as a decent salary. After a speedy telephone interview, I was invited to "come on down." I felt like it was a derby day in the morning. We made arrangements to be on the next bus for Lexington, and from there, on to Houston. Happy surprised me by producing a small hill of extra luggage, all baby clothes specially made by a gaggle of country aunts and cousins who wanted to make sure our baby would be "properly fit up."

The next evening, we arrived at the Shady-A, a small ranch, located in a dusty corner of a rural subdivision outside the city, and surrounded by wildcatter oil rigs. Not pretty! At least the barn, with only ten stalls, had a high roof for a good breeze, and large alleyways. The yard was large, and well organized for the safety of the horses. And the paddock, though a far cry from the manicured perfection of those at Saratoga and Lexington, was tended regularly. One look into the stalls and I knew I was in the company of a string of 'no-hopers' -- just a bunch of nags that might come in third or fourth on a really good day.

My new boss, Barry Howe, was not a trainer I'd ever seen listed in the racing press, but that didn't bother me. The job seemed promising. The salary was a Godsend, with me still owing sizeable monthly payments to the jeweler for a two-carat diamond engagement ring I'd bought Happy -- the only way I could get my girl jockey to abandon the backs of horses for my bed.

Our accommodation had two bedrooms and one bath, with an airy room for the coming baby. Happy headed directly for the bedroom. "Come on darlin'. I'll race ya!" I took off like Arrow flying out of the starting gate. Only faster!

Texas proved good for us. Happy, with her soft Kentucky accent and her all-too-frequent 'home country' words and phrases, was welcomed heartily. She took to the local Baptist community like a homing pigeon. And these Texans didn't treat me as a foreigner just because I'd been born in England. Some of them laughed at my choice of words, and I soon learned to drop the British racing language I'd picked up helping run a stable at Newmarket while studying at Cambridge, especially when I ordered rounds of bourbon and Jack Daniels.

During my first weeks at Barry Howe's ranch, I fell back into the habits of my early days as an intern-trainer, hanging around the local racetrack after early morning gallops.

One dawn, when the Texas sky lived up to its reputation as a glorious jewel, I recognized a trainer I'd known in Kentucky. His name, Heller Burns, seemed to foretell his luck. None!

An alcoholic, Heller had come down in the racing world because of his habit. Like me, he'd become an assistant trainer in a yard of no-hopers.

Fogged by his whiskey breath and strangling his words, Heller slurred, "Good God, Rick! You look terrible. Can't afford a razor? You broke, too?"

I rubbed my chin, and knew I should have spent more time at my washbasin giving my chin another going-over. But I'd gotten into the habit of shaving at night before Happy and I made love, because I didn't want to scratch that delicate skin.

"I've got a job," I said. "Assistant trainer. Married now with a baby on the way. What are you doing down here?" Knowing he was married to his whiskey, I suddenly felt sorry for him, and wished I hadn't mentioned Happy.

"Job? What job?" A double blast of whiskey breath.

"In Howe's yard."

"Nothin' but no-hopers there."

Alluding to what every horse trainer lives for, like a kid on Christmas morning who wants a bicycle from Santa, I said, "You know and I know there's always the chance of a 'miracle'."

"A 'miracle'? Dream on, Brit. Not enough cash among all Barry Howe's owners to buy one. Anyway, he wouldn't know a 'miracle' from a brood mare if he saw one."

"Howe's got a couple of wildcatter owners. They only need to hit one gusher. And, let's face it, oil's always been a winner in the money stakes."

"Them two wildcatters been drillin' for decades." Heller shoved his dirty-mouthed bottle at me.

"Whiskey! At seven in the morning! No thanks," I said to Heller's offer as my stomach churned.

He slurred on, "Now, I'm not sayin' *you* couldn't spot a 'miracle'. What, with your experience at the blueblood yards in Saratoga, all you need is a pocket full'a cash."

Nostalgia hit me like a baseball sent into the stands. I remembered those glorious early morning gallops at the Saratoga racetrack when Happy was a winning girl jockey, and I trained Thoroughbreds. She'd introduced me to the blueberry muffins and cappuccinos served at that track in the early days of our romance. I could almost taste them. We'd be there now, and blissful, if it hadn't been for the triple murders.

Heller stumbled to his dilapidated car, and I wondered if I ought to offer to drive him to his yard before he'd get picked up by the sharp-eyed local police. I did. But he refused the offer.

Later that day, one of our wildcatter owners, Solomon Jones, found me clocking his no-hoper, Gusher. He'd introduced himself with a huge handshake. "Call me Sol." I noticed the oil stains under his fingernails. Didn't matter. I liked him from the word go.

Pointing out his one and only contribution to our string of horses, he mumbled, "Not much, just a nag." Then using his shoulder to bump mine in a friendly way, he added, "I'm drillin' on a new spot. Got a feelin' this is gonna' be the lucky one. And when it shoots up a gusher, I expect to be sendin' you to Kentucky to buy me a decent piece of horse flesh."

"Thanks, Sol. I may be British-born, but I do know my way around the Kentucky yards. Even married a Kentucky girl." Thinking of Happy made my face glow through the emerging after-five stubble. I grew as horny as a teenager. But Happy hadn't been my first great love.

Happy knew I had a longtime relationship with Odette Bailey before we met. Happy had heard all about Odette's terrible lingering leukemia. I was still traumatized by that when Happy surged into my life like the first robin after a cruel winter. Odette and I hadn't married. She hadn't wanted marriage when she was dying. I'd done what I could for poor Odette. Offered to give blood transfusions. Wrong blood type. Traveled the country to find a donor with the suitable bone marrow that could keep her alive. Again, no luck. There were the more mundane tasks: lifting her in and out of the bathtub, the shopping in health food stores to pry out a treat that would tempt her appetite. When Odette died in my arms I thought I'd never go back to a normal life: the life that was normal for me, training horses. It was thanks to finding Happy and her caring, loving heart that my broken self was restored to some semblance of active manhood.

Only days later Solomon Jones struck oil; the black-gold of wildcatters' legends gushed out of the hole for almost two days before it could be capped. With millions in the bank, Sol sent me to Keeneland's next big sale with orders to buy two colts for him. I didn't. I bought one. He named him Nile. And Nile turned out to be a 'miracle'.

Howe's yard was made, and I was once again a trainer who had legitimate hopes.

My baby son Timothy was born healthy, with all his fingers and toes. Bright-eyed but quiet, he awoke in perfect time for me to say goodbye before I left for early morning gallops. Life seemed perfect.

Except that, one morning, Happy's milk dried up. Timothy was screaming and Happy was hysterical. I had to rush to a pharmacy for baby formula, and I walked right into an alleged murder. Yes, *another* death!

2

At the counter, screaming at our local pharmacist, was our next-door neighbor, Mrs. Rawlence. "You killed my husband!" she screeched through racking tears. "You killed him!"

I'm not the kind of husband who hugs other women, but I took Mrs. Rawlence into my arms and cradled her as if she were my infant son in need of tenderness when he's crying.

Mrs. Rawlence sobbed louder. No amount of my hugging was going to offset the loss of Mr. Rawlence. An ordinary sort of woman, with hair the color of dishwater, a flat nose and too-full figure, her only redeeming feature: her nobles' hands. Now they were fluttering like startled butterflies. Worse, they were stained with her husband's blood.

Screeching louder, she repeated her accusation to Oleg, the pharmacist. He had lost most of his non-prescription business to the supermarket down the street. Local gossip had it he was facing hard times.

Through choking tears, Mrs. Rawlence managed to howl, "You killed my Josh! I'm going to sue you until you bleed, like he did from his poor old nose."

Trying to act calm, but with a harsh tone, Oleg countered, "I'll sue YOU for defamation of character, and loss of revenue."

"Josh filled his prescription from you! It's your fault!"

"But he bought his aspirin at the supermarket. If I'd known he was taking a daily aspirin I wouldn't have filled that prescription. I'm a pharmacist, NOT your husband's doctor."

Desperate for baby formula and wondering why I hadn't come home, Happy came into the pharmacy. After I told her what had happened, she dismissed the fact she'd caught me with another woman in my arms. Mrs. Rawlence promptly stopped sobbing, and started to look sheepish, and not because she'd been held in my arms. Over our kitchen sink she'd revealed family secrets to Happy: that her marriage to Josh wasn't exactly idyllic.

"Come home, dear," Happy said, while comforting the woman.

Happy's soft Kentucky accent worked the wonder that my clipped British consonants couldn't offer. Mrs. Rawlence gulped down her accusation and was willingly led, albeit in tears, to our rental car. We bundled her into the front seat for the short ride home.

With Timothy fed and sleeping soundly, Happy sat at our kitchen table, watching for Hyacinth Rawlence to cross our miniscule garden for a neighborly chat. Alone with us, the story came out. She decided to share a few more secrets of Josh's this time.

"My Josh wasn't no ordinary man. As a head security guard at the racetrack he knew things that weren't no laughin' matter. Folks from as far away as Nashville come to see him, offerin' money for info'mation 'bout bettin' scams. He kept his

10

secrets, though, and they cost him his health," she gasped. "And his life!"

As my Happy's one to thirst after a juicy story, I knew they'd be in the kitchen a long, long time.

I offered Hyacinth some fresh coffee. She swallowed it sadly, recalling how her Josh had often swilled coffee in our little kitchen. "Josh was one fine man. Oh, Happy, I know I told you something of our pillowtalk. Wasn't right of me to talk about Josh's peculiar way of havin' sex which I always thought would be the death of him. But if he hadn't taken those damn aspirins with his prescription med'cine, he'd be here today."

"Oh, really?" I said, surprised at Hyacinth's admission that she knew Josh should not have mixed aspirin with his prescription. No wonder she shut up when confronted with that truth at Oleg's pharmacy.

"Hyacinth, sugah, you needn't dwell on that. Got to plan his funeral." Happy poured another coffee for our miserable neighbor. "I know y'all don't attend the Baptist church. Catholic, Irish descent! Must have a wake, too."

Sobbing, Hyacinth went on, "Cain't afford that. Cain't afford no coffin. No burial patch, neither."

More sobs.

Call me a fool, but I made the mistake of offering her what little savings we had. "We'll manage the coffin." Suddenly, we were feeling overwhelmed with Josh's death. Trying to make the best of a possible mistake, Happy added, "Me and my pals'll cook up some food for the wake, and tell everyone to bring their own drinks."

With the plans now set, Hyacinth seemed as normal as ever.

Josh Rawlence's funeral was well attended. No error there, except when the priest called the deceased "Joshua."

"Not Joshua," Mrs. Rawlence yelled out, her voice carrying throughout the church like a bugle call. "Damn you! His name was JOCELYN."

The wake brought more painful moments. Mrs. Rawlence had been tamed for a while until a fiddler came in playing, and with his well-rounded baritone added the opening words, "There's a tall ship standing by." That brought a torrent of tears from Hyacinth Rawlence.

Also in the Irish tradition, a real gypsy had been hired to make an appearance at the door. But this wake wouldn't last a full week, as it would in Ireland. Mrs. Rawlence attacked Josh's doctor as soon as *he* made an appearance in the middle of the wake when everyone's food was still sending up steam.

"You murderer!"

Happy tried to placate Hyacinth, guessing what was coming. "Sugah, don't ... calm yourself."

But there was no placating her this time. Like a cobra spitting its fatal venom, she yelled for all her guests to hear, "You so-called doctor. You killed mah Josh. Poisoned him!"

Josh's doctor wasn't as belligerent as Oleg the pharmacist. Very quietly, through his handlebar mustache, he groaned in his own defense, "Poor Josh. He shouldn't have taken aspirin. Gastric bleeding's always a threat with that prescription. He never told me he was taking aspirin. I could have lessened the dose to reduce the amount of acid produced by the stomach. Next best would have been 'the purple pill' Nexium."

"Just shut up, and gimme back Josh or git outta here. I know you killed him on purpose. I been takin' aspirin all these years too, with no problem."

The doctor bit his lip, leaving a minute dollop of blood there. "Well, Mrs. Rawlence, you are a lady. Uh, I mean, anyways, a woman. And women react differently to aspirin. Woman your age could avoid a stroke by takin' aspirin, though not a heart attack. Men have a reduced risk of a heart attack, but not a stroke when takin' aspirin. But Josh, he had no symptoms of either of those. That's why I never prescribed aspirin for him. Josh died from a hemorrhage. He had poor kidney function. Aggravated his --"

"Damn you! Murderer! Git out!"

Shaking his head causing his mustache to wiggle, the doctor slithered out of the room, carefully avoiding the rough-hewn coffin that was prominently displayed on a borrowed Irish bog-oak table.

Snickers followed him. By trying to rationalize away his responsibility, he had made himself disliked rather than pitied. None of his regular patients came to his defense, either.

When the door clanged behind him, I said, "Aspirin *can* be a poison. I guess the doctor should have taken the time to ask Josh if he took an aspirin every day."

"No doctors take time no more. Ah hates 'em all," a querulous older woman snarled. She had been busily stuffing the bosom part of her dress with finger sandwiches for later. She even had her mouth full while she was snarling.

Not the best of wakes. I felt really relieved when Happy gave me a sign we could leave.

Happy gave her excuse to the other mourners, "Babysitter clocking up the time, and it's well past Tim's dinner hour." Some knew what she meant. Most were too drunk to care.

The babysitter's costly presence was unfortunately replaced by Mrs. Rawlence's sister-in-law, Hilda.

Unwisely, as it turned out, my Happy had extended an invitation to Hilda Rawlence to stay overnight in Timmy's bedroom. She'd come from Boston to Texas for the funeral. She had no intention of staying upstairs with Timmy. She wanted to sit in our kitchen with us.

Hilda proved to be a blabbermouth. She wouldn't go upstairs for an early night. She went on and on about the quality of her brother's coffin, the size of the congregation, the scarcity of flowers.

Happy said quietly, "We really loved Mr. Rawlence. We'll miss him, believe me."

That wasn't good enough for Hilda.

Hilda probed for Happy's past career, before she became a wife and mother.

Sitting easily on the tall stool beside our breakfast counter, Happy said, "Ever since I was twelve, I'd wanted to be a jockey."

"What was stopping you?"

"Only that I lived up in the hills with my Paw. He needed help around the homestead. I'd done my best, ever since Auntie Bessie left us."

"And who was Auntie Bessie?" Hilda's nose twitched like a rat's smelling cheese.

"Paw's sister. My Mama died birthing me. Auntie Bessie had done what she could for me when Paw couldn't cope. Raised me, schooled me 'til I could go to the county school. Taught me to ride, hoe, cook and iron after washing clothes and such. We went to church together. Everything, really."

"But how did that get you to become a jockey?"

"Auntie Bessie left us when I was ten. She fell in love with a Louisville man, Harry Brownlow. Good man, lived at the private stables where he worked. He'd had the same job for years. He was a 'hot walker' - the man who slows down the young horses after gallops. Good job, came with a bungalow on

14

the estate of a horse farm for breeding and racing horses. He told my Auntie Bessie there'd be enough space for three in the bungalow if I slept on the sofa."

"You walked horses. How did that escalate into becoming a jockey?"

"Auntie Bessie, her favorite thing was movies. *National Velvet* was her only video. We saw it over and over. So, when Paw felt I was growing into a woman, what with me getting my period, he sent me to Auntie Bessie for woman talk. Her Harry got me a job at the horse breeding estate where he worked. First off, I walked the horses, same as Harry."

"I still say that's not the same as being a jockey."

"I was a 'hot walker.' When the bosses noticed I could get on with yearlings, I got some riding but not on important horses. That came later."

"You did whatever your Auntie Bessie and Harry told you to do? Very unusual for a teenager. Didn't you rebel after years of sleeping on the sofa?"

"A rebel? Only thing I know to do that has to do with rebels is to give a rebel yell. I'm good at that. Want to hear my rebel yell?"

"No. No thank you. Not tonight, with my brother hardly settled in the ground." Hilda drained the remainder of our coffee from its pot into her cup. "I still can't imagine how you managed to get from 'hot walker' to being a full-time jockey."

"Didn't. Wasn't like that. Anyway, I was never more than an apprentice jockey."

"That's still a big advance from cooling down yearlings."

"Sure was. Didn't happen all at once, either. First off, I helped put bits in their mouths. Be up at six in the morning to help fix their bits. When the yearlings got to know and like me,

I'd put my weight on the body of a yearling without his wearing a saddle. Slow-like, I'd sit up on the yearling's back. In the yard, I'd start working the reins. A groom would put on a saddle when I told him the yearling was ready for that. Many yearlings don't take to the girth. Best to try it out in the yard, never in a stable's stall when the yearling might buck and kick."

"I can hardly believe your skills came naturally."

"None of it was skill. Mostly just hard work. Other riders were plum too scared. Yearlings can sure carry on! But when the bosses saw how I could lead a yearling to the outside schooling area and the yearling stayed real quiet, that's when I started to get riding jobs."

"But to become an apprentice jockey. That was still quite a leap!"

"Yes, Ma'am. But my bosses, they helped me. I got to go to the yearling sales in Keeneland and the big races in Louisville. I watched. I hung around owners clocking horses. I learned. Auntie Bessie, she complained. Said like no nice girl hangs around the track. But she shut up when I got my apprentice license."

Then Hilda turned her wrath on me. "And how come an educated man like you could take up with an apprentice jockey who'd been nothing more than a mountain girl?"

With no hesitation, I snapped back, "I couldn't take my eyes off her wonderful spritely figure, wonderful blue pool-like eyes, wonderful upturned smiling mouth. Happy was sticking around the racetrack like the wrapper on a Mars bar. When I could afford a ring, I winkled her out and proposed."

Hilda Rawlence lifted her shoulders like a prizefighter who had lost on points. "Good night," she spat.

Hilda had put down her empty cup, shrugged away any continued interest in Happy or me, and marched upstairs to Timmy's room.

Finally we could relax in our cozy small bedroom, our welcoming double bed nicely in tandem to our son's cradle, like a mother whale escorting her pup. Then Happy gave me her nightly burlesque routine, teasing me by peeling off her clothes, one by one. But she didn't want to get down to the real treat of being married. "I need to be comforted tonight. I need for you to tell me a story. Not a hog heaven one, please. Somethin' that goes with my miserable mood."

Happy had turned me into a male Scheherazade, telling stories to enhance my marriage. The stories always had to be about racehorses, or about the people who loved them.

I thought fast. What did I know about misery in the racing world? Only the serial murders of the girl jockeys. But Happy, gifted with her very special sixth sense, had been the one to unravel the truth behind *those* murders. She didn't ever want to hear any more about that episode.

Where else to start?

Cuddling under the covers with Happy, and very quiet, so as not to wake up Tim, I began: "Well, there was a young jockey, going down on the train with me to Brighton. I was running a no-hoper there, and he was about to have his first day racing as a jockey. Riding with us in the train compartment were his parents, and his closest friend from the school where he'd just earned his apprentice license."

"How old?"

"Probably all of nineteen, like you, after you'd earned your license." I ventured a hot kiss on her quivering lips. My nether regions were very ready for foreplay, but Happy wanted more of the story, so I obediently continued.

"We traveled down to Brighton all laughs and full of plans for that day's racing. On arrival, a stunning looking girl was waiting on the platform for our newly licensed apprentice jockey. They hugged, kissed and grabbed each other's buttocks in full view of all the other arriving passengers."

I hoped that part of the story might inspire Happy to give mine a squeeze, but no luck.

"Was the girl his fiancée?"

I didn't know about any wedding plans, but they certainly liked the taste of each other. We shared the expense of a taxi to the racecourse. It was a strange sort of day, very foggy like a London pea-soup fog before coal fires were forbidden. The weather didn't faze the two of them; they were at it all the way to the paddock. He went into the jockeys' changing room, aglow from both his sexual joy, and the intense excitement of his first day riding. What's more, this was in an important race."

"The girl? Did she stand at the rails to see what happened?"

"I'm beginning to think I've told you this story before."

"Go on. It's exactly the one I need to hear tonight."

"Yes, Happy. She stood right at the rails, near the finish line, just like a wrestler's wife whose husband's on the ropes, or a bullfighter's fiancée who watches, praying the bull won't gore him. She was there, and she had a prime view. We all saw it from where we stood with her at the rails. He was coming down the stretch, his face alight with joy and the satisfaction of doing what he loved. But then, his mount swerved directly into the rails. They didn't buckle, as they would have at the newer racecourses where rails are made of plastic. Those rails might as well have been made of Cotswold stone. My new friend was thrown. His neck was broken instantly. End of story. End of him. End of what had promised to be a lovely day and a great career."

"Oh Rick, come on and hold me close. I need you darlin', I need your lovin'."

Forget foreplay. The story did that work for me. And soon Happy was making so much noise she woke Tim up. I stretched out my arm into his crib and found that he had wet through his diaper, pajamas and sheets.

Happy's lovemaking had left her exhausted; she'd turned over and fallen fast asleep. Nothing left for me but to change Tim. Smelly job. I was rewarded with one of his newly emerging smiles. Wonderful.

Our sheets were wet through too. But I liked that smell.

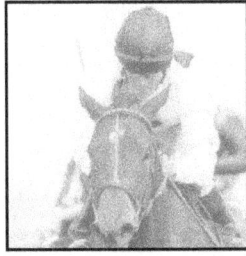

3

I told Happy the next day before early morning gallops, "A good trainer wins when he chooses the race for a horse. That's why I'm glad we're going to Arlington. That track has the best surface for Nile."

"Maybe the track's great for Nile, but isn't Chicago known as the Windy City? Maybe that's not so safe for Timothy."

"Tim will be fine. There are plenty of babies in Chicago. We'll be there for the races in mid-August when the weather's great."

"Arlington's pretty late in the racing season. Won't Nile get raced before?"

Happy felt back in her element; I know, because her lips were in the ecstatic crescent they took on whenever racing or racecourses loomed on her horizon. The next day, she was up at the crack of dawn, busily packing Timothy's things. An awful lot of clothes and accessories: buggy, collapsible bath, diaper bags. She was the world's best mother.

Barry Howe had decided to send us ahead to scout out the track's possibilities for Nile. Sol was paying all the fees, our expenses in Chicago at a top hotel, and had even added a bonus to my regular salary. I felt no omen of disaster approaching.

Just gratitude, and anticipation of more blessings seemed to be in the offing.

I concurred with Barry's plan for Nile. As a two-year-old, he was to have a light racing season. Maybe only one race. One he could most certainly win. One at a track which guaranteed he wouldn't take a disliking to racing early on.

At our home track we'd trained him to accept the starting gates. We'd run him on ground that was heavily watered. No damage was to harm his hooves. No colossal noise must break his concentration, as was rumored to have caused Devon Loch to lose the Grand National with Dick Francis in the saddle wearing the Queen Mother's colors.

Our Nile had the pick of the nation's two-year-olds' races. But Barry had eliminated every race except one at Arlington. "Right distance for his breeding. Right shape of track. And his sire had won there," he said, wisely.

"You know, Happy, it's a strange thing how the magic nick can work out. In racehorse breeding, so often it's neither the sire nor the dam or a horse's immediate past that ends up counting. It's that special something that forces its way through the barriers of breeding to exert its magical influence. A grand-dam four or five generations back can nick just right with a sire that's unpopular and has bargain basement nicking scores. Nile's a prime example of that. I bought him cheap in Keeneland. But just watch, he's a 'miracle,' I can feel it."

"I feel it, too, darlin'. I'll be cheerin' louder than anyone at the finish line." And she did.

Nile won his Arlington race with eight lengths to spare. Barry, Sol and I spontaneously threw our arms around each other. Happy would have been part of our circle of joy, but with her sixth 'horse' sense, she was already waiting for Nile to come into the winner's circle. Nile could have won by more but

I'd cautioned his jockey to give him an easy race. Also, I didn't want the quick-buck hunting punters to know just how good he really is. I'd been extra cautious to give special instructions to our jockey after seeing the disaster that robbed Powerscourt of 'The Million' at Arlington.

I recalled how we'd stood under the great overhang at the Arlington grandstand to watch Mrs. John Magnier's Powerscourt come in first at the finish line. A smallish son of great Sadler's Court, he was cheered down the 10-furlong stretch by no less than some twenty-eight thousand viewers. A white flag went up. "Hold all tickets" came the announcement over the microphone. The Stewards decided that his jockey, Jamie Spencer, had allowed his mount to take an errant position, swerve in the late stages of the race, and impede his rivals. So, his Ireland-based trainer, Aidan O'Brien, had to swallow pride because his wonder horse was taken down from the top spot.

I made sure that didn't happen to Nile.

When Nile won his race, big-time trainers crowded into the winners' circle to congratulate me, and invite me to parties in their homes and yachts on the lake. But Happy didn't trust the babysitters in Chicago, so I had to stay home with her and our son. No way would I have left Happy to play nursemaid while I followed her dream, consorting with top trainers and owners from all corners of the U.S. and Europe.

However, invitations that included Happy and Timothy came later from four trainers.

From Southern California's Santa Anita track came Bono Munoz, a Latino who knew more about polo ponies than racehorses. From Arkansas came Colin Whitey. Nice guy, no dress sense, Colin arrived at a racecourse looking like he was headed for the beach. We got on fine. I think I was the only

Englishman he'd ever met and he thought it was a fun thing to know a real Brit. From Belmont in New York came Lawrence van der Holt, who remembered me from the girl-jockey murders fiasco. He was an elegant guy, dressed in a different Brooks Brothers blazer and slacks every day, to suit the weather. He made a play for Happy. She had a cigarette in her fingers at the time and simply put it out in his hand. That stopped him from trying anything further.

From Dubai came Hassan Massoud, an Iraqi who had settled in Dubai because racing had taken off so brilliantly there. It has one of the newest and most comfortable tracks in the world: The Nad Al Sheba Racecourse, located only ten minutes from downtown, and with the top money prize of $6 million for its major race. The best horses in the world now go there and I wondered if it might suit Nile.

I asked Hassan Massoud about that race. He explained it suited three-year-olds that could handle its two chutes, gradual left-hand turns before entering a 600-meter finishing straight. He also said its 2000-meter chute would be used for the World Cup. The track is made up of a hard-dirt base with 18 inches on its surface, of which 8 inches is regularly harrowed up; and the track is well-drained, and state of the art equipment is used to seal the surface in the unlikely event of a rainfall."

Perfect. Dubai would be perfect for Nile, once I'd trained him up to that distance. The climate could be too hot for some horses, but most loved it. And the stables were air conditioned.

We started out on a first-name basis - Rick and Hassan - and felt a certain familiarity. I didn't think I'd ever see him again after Arlington, but I did.

Hassan spoke with an Oxford English accent. He had studied at Oxford, and had worked hard on the accent. He could

24

have almost passed for a Brit, except he wore clothes that didn't fit well and he ate garlic; two social no-nos. His hair was permanently greased like a well-oiled engine, and his lips may have been a rosy color; I think he used cosmetics, at least blusher and lip gloss. He took Happy and me to the Pump Room, Chicago's ultra-expensive restaurant, and arranged to have a nanny for Timothy. When Happy went to the ladies' room, he suggested something that took me by surprise.

"Rick, old chap. When will we have the pleasure of your company in Dubai? I've got a woman there I'd like you to meet. You wouldn't believe how tasty she is. Better than a truffle. I'll hand her over to you, all expenses paid. And believe me, she'll give you the ride of your life!"

"No thanks, Hassan. I'm married to a wonderful girl."

"So am I, old chap. What has that got to do with having a little ride on the side? A great bonk is a great bonk! You'll see what I mean when you get to Dubai. And you can return the favor by introducing me to the owners. But not those in your yard."

'Why?', I wondered. Then figured he was just curious about my newfound success.

Trainers: they come in all types, and sizes. What I didn't expect was to watch while so many of them were murdered. That's right, murders, again!

4

My little family's return to Texas was far from being filled with delights as our outward bound trip had been.

Tim had a nasty cold. Happy had overheard some of Hassan's pimping, and was withholding lovemaking. "You should've told him to shut up!" she growled at me.

Should have, would have, but I hadn't, and was now aching to be back in Happy's arms.

Things were even dreary at early morning gallops. Heller Burns, in a drunken stupor, had crashed his car and died instantly. We'd actually grown quite friendly over the months before he died.

I missed his racing stories, although they'd been told in a fog of whiskey breath. I'd relayed lots of them to Happy, and had been rewarded by delicious lovemaking in return.

I'd told him what I believed made a great racehorse. A big behind that powers the back legs. Good withers. Conformation doesn't matter if he isn't a hurdler. Short neck, long neck, fifteen or seventeen hands, all that doesn't matter either if the horse likes racing and wants to win.

Heller agreed, except he believed a trainer should look into a horse's eyes. "Read in a book once, about that Ian Home Dudgeon fella' who won the Olympics equestrian medal for

Ireland. Book told how this Dudgeon guy would peer into a horse's eyes and know what the horse was thinkin'."

"Eyes do tell you a lot," I agreed. "I looked into Mill Reef's eyes once, in Paris, just before he won the Arc de Triomphe race. Powerful little guy. He'd also won the Derby and the King George and Queen Elizabeth. But he was so small that when he went to work as a stallion, a trench had to be dug for the mares to be placed in, or else he wouldn't have managed to cover them. Didn't matter. His eyes revealed his greatness in both the racing and covering departments."

Heller and I had both been around plenty of tracks, and knew what racing was all about.

At least, I thought I did.

Then I got a verbal kick in the stomach. Sol telephoned to say he was buying race cars now instead of racehorses. Worse, much worse, he said: "And I'm movin' to California, takin' Nile with me. He's goin' to Bono Munoz's yard for training."

The news hit Barry like a lightning bolt. Except for Nile, all his other runners were no-hopers.

My career was salvaged when Sol added, "I'm givin' Nile to Bono on the condition he takes you on as assistant trainer." Done deal, we were moving to Los Angeles.

Happy didn't want to move. She worried about Hyacinth Rawlence, who had no other close friend to help her through her bereavement. She lamented: "Poor woman has no one else to swear around. Since she lost her law case against the doctor, she uses all that awful language around me 'cause she don't -- I mean doesn't -- dare say damn and shit and all those words around anyone else. She needs to say them. It's her way of grieving and gettin' it all out."

"Lost the case? I hadn't heard that!"

"Yeah! Lost! With no chance of appeal. The Judge said the doctor's claim was right, that Josh had brought on his death by self-medicating hisself -- darn, I mean himself."

"Happy, we've got to think of our future now. You'll make new friends in California." I hung out that carrot: "You love the movies, and you'll meet movie stars."

She took the bait.

"Real, honest-to-God movie stars? Hog heaven! And the climate's better in California for Tim. He won't do so much sweatin' in the summer. He's had a cold all autumn. Okay, darlin', let's give that climate a chance."

No contest. Anyway, I hadn't a choice. Barry couldn't afford to keep me on with nothing but no-hopers in his yard. It was California and Bono, or poverty again.

5

By January, 2006, we'd made the move. At first, Los Angeles seemed very promising. Bono leased a decent cottage for us in Beverly Glen Canyon -- half way between the San Fernando Valley and the west side. It had air conditioning, which our place in Texas lacked.

Tim soon got over his cold.

Our cottage was down the street from where Marilyn Monroe had lived and died. There were still two living, breathing ancient movie stars on our street. Happy got busy collecting movie star memorabilia, and managed to buy some nice dresses and matching handbags the two old stars had worn in their movies so long ago.

Our lovemaking was delicious in the air conditioned bedroom with its built-in TV. I'm ashamed we watched a bit of porn, although it was like taking coals to Newcastle. Happy and I didn't really need that.

There were only two glitches during our time in L.A.

The first was that Nile was beginning to disappoint Bono due to his different training practices.

But not me. Bono knew that Nile had won his only race at seven furlongs. "He's nothing but a speed merchant," Bono declared when he clocked Nile's gallops at his first outing on

California turf. "Maybe he could win a sprint again over seven furlongs, but no classic race. He needs to go a mile or a mile and a quarter."

Of course I knew that. I'd intended to first school Nile over a mile, and hoped by autumn he could win at a mile and a quarter. Both his sire and dam had won over a mile and a quarter. Why shouldn't he? I didn't argue with Bono about the colt's distance. What was the use? Bono's Latin eyes threw sparks of anger, and his thick lips curled with sneers. No use barking at him. I'd only lose my job.

With a newly-transported wife and infant to support, I couldn't afford the luxury of a confrontation.

The second glitch was that I didn't trust Bono. Not because of his opinion on the colt's distance, but because he'd poached Nile and Sol from Barry's yard. I considered that 'dirty horse pool.'

For the moment there was nothing I could do; so, like a harried teacher threatened by teenage students, I swallowed my words.

Poor Happy, she was the one on the receiving end of my black moods. The only way out for her was to have sex often. No complaints from Happy. But she soon became pregnant again.

This time, pregnancy wasn't so easy: morning sickness, fainting, and a spotty complexion might have dampened her spirits. But no, she chirped over and over: "I bet I'm gonna have a girl this time, Rick. She'll have your British nose and my figure. I mean, the figure I used to have before gettin' pregnant. Bet she'll be a movie star."

Most pregnant women have cravings for special foods. Not my Happy. Her craving was for more and more racing stories. She ate them up!

6

Racing stories. How Happy loved those tales of great horses and owners of days gone by! Like a male Scheherazade, I provided stories that would keep our love alive while she was in a family way, again. But this time I started with a news story about a famous jockey who was retiring to stay at home with his wife and kid.

"Remember seeing Jerry Bailey ride?" I began.

"Sure 'nuf. He won over 5,800 races."

"Yes, and had 30,000 starts, retiring at the top of his career at only 48 years old. Nowhere near the age when Lester Piggott retired. Jerry started at that little track, Sunland Park, in New Mexico, way back in 1974. He told me, when we were still in Florida, 'I never really thought I was any more special than anyone else out there. I can't believe how lucky I've been. Hell, I never expected to get out of New Mexico.' Bailey's son Justin is thirteen. The beginning of that chancy time for kids. He figures Justin needs a father figure and he's crazy about his wife, Suzee, who wants him to become a TV racing analyst. I don't know why she wanted him to retire; he's never had a major injury in twenty years. But there's no doubt he'd be a great television announcer. You know, I read his book, *Against the Odds: Riding for my Life*."

"I've read it too. My favorite part is how he got two Kentucky Derby wins, and won three Kentucky Oaks."

"Yes. And four victories in the Dubai Cup, five in the classic Breeders' Cup and six times on horses that got the Triple Crown. Add to that seven Eclipse Awards as the nation's top jockey. Even as a kid starting in 1974, his first year as a jockey, he had nine victories in sixty-six starts. It was miraculous how he won ten races out of ten starts with Cigar in 1995."

"And don't forget when Bailey was riding Arcangues in the BC Classic, and won at 133-to-one odds. In all he earned $295 million in American purses."

Happy had begun to finish my stories even more frequently, which let me know she missed jockeying. Her injury in Saratoga put a stop to that. To compensate she followed all the jockeys' stats and foibles.

I said, "He made another $5 million in races in other countries."

"But he lost on his last ride. He was on that six-year-old chestnut. I saw the whole thing on TV. It was at Cleverland Farm, the Turf Stakes, a mile and a quarter race. Bailey wanted to tuck in behind the leaders, and wait to make his move. He got trapped behind a wall of horses and was beaten by three quarters of a length by a 48-1 long shot named Miesque's Approval."

"In his book, Bailey said, 'I didn't get to my spot as early as I needed to. I got blocked and had nowhere to go. I had a feeling it was going to be too little too late.'"

"That's right. I read his comments on the race in his book, too." Then, I sighed, and repeated one of my favorite expressions, "That's racing."

The telephone rang. I left Happy and Tim cuddling and took the call in the kitchen.

The call was from Epsom, a small town in Surrey, not far from London.

"Rick, it's Ivor Wren, remember me? I've been looking for you all over America to be my assistant trainer. Any interest in coming back to England?"

"Ivor! Good to hear your voice. Hold on a minute. I'll have a word with my wife. Sounds interesting!"

I rushed back into our bedroom. Tim was asleep. Happy tenderly lifted her fingers to her lips to warn me to "be quiet." I waited while she lay Tim between his sheets, lowered the light, and then I pulled her into the hall.

"Happy, you won't believe it! My luck's back! It's my old school chum, Ivor Wren on the phone. Quite a successful trainer with a good stable in Epsom, and he trains his horses on the course. He asked me to join him as assistant trainer. What do you say?"

Happy sucked in her breath, and paused, not giving a thought to what the long distance call might cost Ivor. When she finally spoke it was with great concentration. "Good schools in England for Tim. I suppose we could make a go of it. I often think of the time we spent at Ascot with Arrow and Attila; that was wonderful. How much is this Ivor goin' to pay?"

Happy, the astute Kentucky wife: Money, first!

"I'm not sure, yet. We didn't get that far." She frowned, and said, "Wait, you haven't been that pleased with Bono and how he's training Nile, you havin' to be polite 'n all that. I know how hard it's been for you, darlin'." She paused to think. "Take the job with Ivor. I'll back you the best I can."

No further discussion. It was to be Ivor's stables and Epsom! I dashed back to the phone to let Ivor know our decision. He was overjoyed!

When I gave Bono my notice, there wasn't much good will on either side. I didn't get a parting bonus: not even a handshake. I packed up my things, said a sad goodbye to Nile, thinking how this good horse could have been made into a *great* horse, and went to the nearest travel agent to arrange our trip to England.

We arrived at Gatwick Airport on an extremely cold morning. Happy had brought a huge collection of baby clothes, which was just as well because he'd need layers in this climate.

I rented a car from Avis at the airport and drove directly to Epsom, which was only a few miles away. We hoped the cottage would at least be warmed for our arrival. It was welcoming. Not only did it have excellent central heating, just recently installed, but there were two fireplaces with blazing logs burning. Its thatched roof helped to retain the heat as well. Though I hadn't lived in England for almost eight years, the cottage was better than I would have thought possible.

Ivor Wren, a handsome bloke, was waiting for us in our small drawing room, holding up an open bottle of scotch.

"Let's celebrate, old chum," and there was a Coca Cola for Happy. But Ivor's best surprise was that he'd hired a nanny for Tim as part of the deal.

The nanny, Mrs. Roe, took over immediately, giving us all orders as to where we were to put our things and what we were to eat for lunch. The cottage had two bathrooms: one with a hand basin and toilet, the other even simpler with only one huge tub. She had placed a bouquet of field flowers on the table, but offered no sweet smile. "I'm Mrs. Roe," she announced between orders. Tim was now *her* charge, not *ours*.

Happy accepted Mrs. Roe for what she was. "Very English," she whispered to me, nodding in the nanny's direction. I nodded in return, while wondering if Mrs. Roe was going to dominate Happy's life from this day forward. No worry. She didn't.

Ivor and I proceeded to sip our scotch, and fill the rest of the day with "horse talk," past, present and future.

While I settled in at Ivor's yard familiarizing myself with the horses, grooms and stable lads, Happy made friends with the lady of the manor house on the hill above our cottage. She was very grand.

Her name was Eleanor Grace, the 38-year-old granddaughter of an Earl, but with no title because her father was the Earl's younger son. I didn't need to explain all those formalities of British peerage to Happy because she had acquired a new copy of Debrett's, which listed all the current peers, their descendants and heirs.

Ellie, as our non-titled neighbor preferred to be called, took Happy in hand as tyrannically as Mrs. Roe had taken over Tim's life.

In her aristocratic but gravelly voice, Ellie commanded, "First, we must rid you of that Kentucky accent. I've booked you for elocution lessons. Then we'll have to do something about your clothes. Oh, I've nothing against thrift-shop apparel, but if you're going to wear 'second-hand,' it *must* have been worn by a celebrity. I know just the shop to fit you out."

Thanks to Ellie, Happy soon could pass for a former student of Heathfield, the snobby English girls' school. Her clothes fit exquisitely, although I didn't like it that her skirts were so short the grooms down at Ivor's yard took to whistling whenever she stopped by. But the biggest blessing to my ears was her much-improved use of the English language. In public there were not more 'ain'ts' or double negatives, drawls or twangs.

If my little Happy, like a butterfly emerging from its chrysalis, underwent a metamorphosis, so did Ellie. Her gravelly voice softened, she now walked with a feminine grace. Ellie had met Ivor through us, and they'd fallen in love.

We were in Tim's nursery, enjoying Mrs. Roe's day off, when Ellie burst in to tell us how wonderful it was to be in love. "I feel like I'm swimming in warm water all day!"

When Happy interrupted, Ellie hardly listened to her question. "Ellie, what shall I wear to Royal Ascot?"

Ellie looked up at the ceiling, staring, as if a portrait of Ivor were hanging there looking down at her. "Ivor has such divine brown eyes. Nobody in my family has brown eyes. A first! When we have children will they have brown eyes? What's Mendel's Law have to say about that?"

"Ellie! Focus! Royal Ascot! Will the hats have big brims or be perched over one eye?"

"I wonder what Ivor looks like in a top hat? I didn't go up to York last season for the Ascot races that were moved there. None of us did. But now that the new stands are completed, we'll all be going back to Royal Ascot. Tell me, Rick. Will Ivor's stable have horses running at Ascot? I shan't go, if Ivor isn't there."

I watched Happy rolling her eyes, then she told Ellie exactly what she wanted to hear. "We've several horses running at Ascot."

I said, "Yes, Ivor should be overseeing them. As for me, I may have to go to Ireland, where there's a good race that week for a horse I particularly like."

"Ireland?" Happy wailed. "Not Ascot? Now that I've acquired proper speaking skills, and bought so many clothes for the occasion?"

Ellie remained in her besotted state, staring at the ceiling. "My grandfather said, in the old days, trainers didn't even wear top hats and tailcoats at Ascot. He said trainers wore jodhpurs and puttees. Ivor would look great in anything, even jodhpurs."

But when Ascot week arrived, it wasn't Ivor overseeing our horses. I stood in for him. Because Ivor was dead! Killed by a shotgun in his home. And it was Ellie, who'd only moved in with him one week earlier, who found him.

Oh God! Another murder? Not Ivor! Dead, yes! But this time, it was death by his own hand.

7

She'd heard a shotgun go off, and thought Ivor had potted a pheasant, or taken a shot at an intruder. Dashing downstairs, Ellie found Ivor in a pool of his own blood. Hysterical, grieving, like the widow she wasn't, Ellie burst into our kitchen and gulped out what she'd seen. "Blood! Blood on everything! Curtains, paintings, mirrors and on the sofa. Ivor had propped up the gun on the sofa, knelt in front if it, then blew his . . . Oh God! I can't, I can't go on!"

The neighbors must have heard the shot, Ellie's screams, and called 911 because the ambulance arrived almost immediately.

Happy cuddled Ellie as if she were a baby. "We'll go to church," Happy said, "and pray for him."

I was in shock, and couldn't utter a word. But I knew more than I could say. Weeks before, Ellie had lured Happy to join the Church of England, giving the excuse there was no Baptist congregation anywhere near our home. Like a swan among ducks, Happy had transferred her allegiance and piety very promptly.

Ellie howled, "No church! No prayers! I want to do some good in this world. No more primping or prowling the resale shops, or trying on hats for Royal Ascot. I'm going to dedicate myself to the poor, and devote myself to community service. Like St. Francis, I'm giving up the trappings of wealth to serve the less fortunate."

But I kept my thoughts to myself, given the situation at hand. I wondered how long Ellie's declarations would last.

Alone in our kitchen, after we'd tucked Ellie into the spare bed in the attic room, I told Happy what really happened to Ivor.

Ivor had a recurring headache and complained to his doctor about stomach cramps. Severe ones. Increasing, all the time. Ivor had tried aspirin, and when that didn't help, he asked the doctor if he could have cancer. The doctor said no, but Ivor must not have believed him. He was convinced he was dying, as the pain became intolerable. That's why he shot himself. What's more, he didn't want Ellie to know."

Happy shook her curls, now swept back into waves behind her ears like the late Princess Diana's when she was still HRH and alive.

A few tears trickled down Happy's cheeks.

Still a practical mountain girl from Kentucky at heart, she asked quietly, "What happens to us now? Will we be able to stay here?"

"Yes, my darling. Before Ivor did this terrible deed, he placed me in charge. His wealthy Canadian owner, Hal Murphy, who owns this estate, wants me to continue with the plans, with or without Ivor. His horse, Anchor, is a good prospect to win the top sprint race."

Happy asked, "What about Ivor's house? Do we have to move in? I prefer it here. Better heating. Ivor's place was always freezing. I never dared to take Timothy there."

"We won't be moving into his house," I reassured her. "I was fond of Ivor, and knew him since our school days when we played rugby. I've been too entrenched with the horses to have met any of the owners. So it's very important that I get his list of owners tomorrow morning. I'll have to go in there tomorrow to collect all the paperwork for the stables. I'll be calling them with the sad news."

Timothy was just over one year old and taking his first steps. He could say "Mama," and RaeRae for Mrs. Roe, but hadn't learned to say "Papa." My fault. I'd spent so many daylight hours with the horses in the yard, the paddock and at the race track.

Like learning the differences between Coca Cola, Pepsi Cola and Crown Cola, I'd needed to study the characteristics of the racehorses in our stable. Had the costly alterations at Ascot included superior drainage so that they could perform at their peak? I'd heard that they included cambers to make the track more comfortable for horses at full racing speed. A world class racing surface was being advertised. But could our mudders handle the going when it was firm? Would it be as right as it had previously been? I prayed so.

Ellie didn't disappoint Happy. She was a loyal friend. From day one Ellie picked Happy up in her Bentley so they could go to the 'Riding for the Disabled' stables where Happy was ecstatic to meet Princess Anne, the Queen's daughter. They also visited soup kitchens where the two girls doled out food to the homeless. At a hospice they covered their resale celebrity clothes with cotton aprons.

Happy was in her element, like a Big Sister from her Baptist community church.

The old injury to Happy's right hand had completely healed so she was also able to become an instructor at the 'Riding for the Disabled' charity, and helped at their events.

My primary job had been to keep our owners content. With his no-hoper competing at Beverly, I'd stood beside a Yorkshireman whose broad accent matched the too-new shoes he wore.

At Doncaster, our stable star Broadback won for his sophisticated owner, Colonel Flyte. His shoes were at least thirty years old, from Lobbs, with bare patches on the suede. A younger son of some minor Baron, he prided himself on being permitted to use the title of Colonel before his surname, because he'd fought in the Korean war in the 1950's.

He addressed me as a minion from the pre-parade ring: "You there! What the hell really happened to Ivor? Coward's way out? Shot himself! I heard it from another trainer who called me from Dubai the day after. Some Iraqi called Hassan Massoud. Know him?"

"Yes, Colonel." I always addressed people by the titles they crave to hear, even that fake Baroness, Penny Blow, who murdered the three jockeys at Saratoga. "Met Hassan at Arlington, when Nile won."

"I remember the Nile story," he said, "how Bono Munoz stole Nile away, and lured his owner to Los Angeles with the promise to get him fast race cars. Well, won't happen with me. I'm the loyal sort. Conservative Party. Church of England. That is, unless you make a mess of Broadback's career. Then you can be damned sure I'll get another trainer."

That day, when Broadback won his Doncaster race, there was no offer of a whiskey or champagne from Colonel Flyte. Just a gruff, "Course suits him here. Now you better get him ready for the St. Leger!"

That was a very tall order. The St. Leger being the last of the possibilities for an English Triple Crown. No way would Broadback win the first two stages, the Two Thousand Guineas at Newmarket, and the Derby at Epsom. I made a note to bring Broadback to Doncaster again, but for a small race.

Royal Ascot week opened on an extremely hot, sultry Tuesday. It had been decades since Berkshire's ground had been baked from so much heat and sun. Happy dressed sublimely in a sweet silk printed mini with a huge Scarlett O'Hara style straw *chapeau* trimmed in matching silk. She sat forward in our rental car to spare her skirt from being wrinkled. Her eyes swept the forest of ancient trees that preceded her first look at the new stands at Ascot. There were rhododendrons climbing in front of the trees, and dense foliage that all but screened the racecourse.

"Wow! Lookee there!" Happy chortled: "All those folks having to walk to the course to save those awfully high fees for parking: one hundred and fifty pounds! Thank God we've got free parking in the owners' and trainers' lot. And those girls, teetering on their five-inch heels. I wonder if they'll even make it to the front gates."

I followed her pointing finger. Shouldn't have. Should have kept concentrating on the road. I came close to scratching an antique 1929 Rolls Royce. Its uniformed chauffeur made a rude two-fingers-up-yours sign to me.

There were queues for everything. Queues to enter the racecourse. Queues to enter the High Street. Queues to find a place in our car park. Queues to get in line to have Happy's pocketbook and my binocular case examined by security personnel.

Happy joined the queue for the ladies' toilets, and frowned because in line she saw another woman wearing her same printed silk dress. Luckily, that woman's hat was of the tiny variety, perched over one eye. Otherwise maybe Happy would have stayed in the toilets until it was time for the first race.

We joined Bill and his wife, Bea for a sandwich in the least grand of Royal Ascot's watering spots. It faced the course, but could have been any new-style pub in London, with minimalist chairs and plastic-topped tables. After a bear hug for me from Bill, and two air kisses for Happy from Bea, I was asked if I knew an Hassan Massoud. Bill added, "A muslim with an Oxford accent. He wondered if I needed a trainer. I told him pretty quick I had a damned good one called Rick Harrow."

Funny, when you hear about a person, then for a long period, nothing, then you see him days later. I was in the pre-parade ring at Royal Ascot for the first fillies' race, when Hassan Massoud greeted me effusively, with his Oxford accent and pompous manner. He generated a lot of warmth; maybe from Dubai's desert. He was overseeing the saddling up of a promising looking filly. "Rick Harrow, what a pleasure!"

"Hello, Hassan. Good looking filly . . ."

"For horse flesh, sure. But you should get a taste of the human filly I'm riding at the moment. I'm willing to share her, with you."

"No thanks. I told you at Arlington, I love my wife."

"And I told you that has nothing to do with a good lay."

My head groom led out our stable's filly. I took the reins and walked away from Hassan.

Wouldn't you know he won that race? Beat our filly into second place.

That night, warm under the covers in our bed, I didn't mention seeing Hassan to Happy. I remembered how upset she'd been over his last offer to me. Instead we had glorious lovemaking and afterwards I told her a story. Happy always

48

wanted a story, but this one may have seemed too close to what had happened to Ivor.

"Have you heard of a great American racing family by the name of Woodward?"

Happy reverted to her Kentucky-style of speaking. "Sho 'nuf. I've seen that name on lists of owners in both the States and here."

"Did you ever hear how Ann Woodward shot her husband to death?"

Short silence. "No. And maybe I don't want to."

"It's quite a story. Dominick Dunne wrote a novel based on it called *The Two Mrs. Grenvilles*. Changed their names. A movie was made, too. And Truman Capote penned a nasty book, *Answered Prayers*. Quite a story."

Happy couldn't resist the bait. "Tell it to me."

"My father met the elder Mr. Woodward at a race. The Woodwards had Captain Boyd-Rochfort as their trainer, the step-father of Henry Cecil. He trained for some of America's top owners and Brits like the Cayzers and the Wyatts. The Woodwards won important trophies on both sides of the pond. But Mrs. Ann Woodward was no trophy wife. In fact, she was never really the wife of William Woodward, having entered into a bigamous union with him, her first husband being still alive."

"So how come she didn't shoot the first husband instead of Mr. Woodward?"

"Ask her! Only, you can't , because she killed herself in 1975 after reading excerpts of Truman Capote's book in *Esquire Magazine*. One character was based on Ann being guilty of the murder, although a New York grand jury acquitted her three weeks after the shooting."

"What did the police think?"

"She told the police and the press that she'd been warned there were burglars operating in her vicinity, so she'd kept a shotgun beside her bed. When she heard footsteps outside her door, and moved into the corridor opposite her husband's bedroom door, it suddenly opened and she shot blindly, believing she was stopping a thief. Instead, she killed husband number two."

"And the police believed her?"

"Not entirely. The police began their investigations. They said they wanted to interview any known burglars caught during that time frame. Their Suffolk County colleagues came up with Paul Widths; then, a Nassau detective, Edward Currant, stepped in. He said, 'The police out there turned Widths over to us. We took him to the Woodwards' house. He admitted he was in the house when he heard two shots, but ran away quickly, hid in a barn, and that on his way into the house, he'd broken the limb of a tree when climbing to reach a window. After he got in he said he hid in a closet that had a safe. We checked and found the broken tree limb, and the closet with the safe. You couldn't do much better than that!'"

"So she got off because the police believed this Paul Widths. But what if he'd been paid by Ann Woodward to make up the story, and *she* broke the tree limb?"

"That's a possibility. She'd employed private detectives for seven years to trail her husband because she believed he was having affairs. They discovered he'd been dating as many as ten women. Ann was afraid she might get dumped without alimony; especially if it was disclosed she was a bigamist. So, murdering her husband cost her no more than two cartridges in a shotgun."

"I sure don't like the sound of that."

"She could have told her private detective to come up with a known burglar who could be bought."

"Why did she pick that particular night? Because of the warnings of burglars in the vicinity?"

"You've got that right. It was in late October 1955, the night before Halloween, and the Woodwards had been invited to a society function honoring the Duchess of Windsor. Fifty-eight guests were wined and dined by Edith Baker, widow of an influential banker, at her Locust Valley home. William Woodrow was then thirty-five. Ann was four years older. They had two sons William III, eleven, and James, seven. Keep their ages in mind. William III was conceived when his father was only twenty-two. Ann was already a tough ex-model and showgirl."

"Sure 'nuf."

" Born in Kansas on a farm, she'd had a hard climb up the social ladder. Interestingly, her husband's family had never accepted her before the shooting. Yes, I said *before* the shooting. William's mother was of the highest ranking social set, born an Ogden and a Cryder. She decided to protect the Woodward name for her grandsons' future by defending Ann, and claiming that her daughter-in-law was innocent. I don't know that Ann's sons really believed in her innocence. They were both at home at the time of the gunning down of their father. One of them killed himself years later."

"Rick! This *is* a terrible story."

"It gets worse, from a trainer's point of view. Imagine how William's trainer felt. That was the same year his best horse, Nashua was considered the greatest in America. And then his owner dies - murdered! You and I both know how difficult it is for a trainer to get owners, especially owners who can buy potentially great horses."

"From a wife's point of view, I don't understand how Ann didn't recognize her husband's footsteps. A wife knows her husband's footsteps."

"Yes, and moreover he was nude. A wife would know her husband when he's nude, his smell, his posture. How could she have thought a burglar was prowling around naked!"

"Did Ann inherit his money?"

"The Woodwards' lawyer said she'd get millions. But more important to Ann was if New York society would readmit her. Then Truman Capote's book came out."

"Wow. Let's not have any guns in *our* house, Rick. I couldn't bear to lose you."

"Or I, you."

With those words we fell asleep in each other's arms.

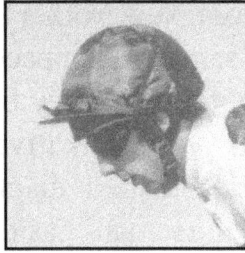

8

During Royal Ascot week I had two pleasant surprises. First, I noticed what a good impression my Happy made on our owners. The elocution lessons and gorgeous celebrities' clothing paid off. Second, I was greeted by three trainers who'd been friendly to us at Arlington. And now *we* had a home to invite *them* to for dinner.

Happy didn't serve grits and hushpuppies with fried chicken. Mrs. Roe helped her cook a decent leg of lamb, and make a proper mint sauce - watery and bitter. For dessert, which was one of England's favorites, she produced a pudding known by the name of 'spotted Dick' among others. Happy complained about the name Mrs. Roe called it, but she downed it with good grace.

One guest was trainer Colin Whitey from Arkansas. His clothes were all wrong again, but in the paddock at Ascot he'd worn a perfect morning coat hired from Moss Brothers, who would never have permitted him to make a monkey of himself. That tailcoat was the correct black and the trousers striped.

I'm not sure but I bet Whitey would have preferred grits and hushpuppies to the thin gray slices of lamb. He must have felt out of place and a long way from home because he had a sorry expression like a dog who misses his master.

Another guest from New York's Belmont was Lawrence van der Holt. His dress sense was impeccable, and he arrived at our home in a perfectly tailored navy blue suit. He seemed in his element, and was very talkative. "An accomplished trainer's like a doctor...a skilled diagnostician. I've always believed that a talented horseman 'has the eye' and can guess a yearling's future. You, Rick, demonstrated that when you chose Nile as a yearling. And speaking of Nile, what's happening to Bono? Isn't he here at Ascot? I haven't seen his name on many race cards."

"He refused to retrain Nile to race as a miler, so he'd never get a mile and a quarter out of him. No classic possibilities for him here. Bono has mostly no-hopers, other than Nile, in his yard."

"In any case, it's very difficult to get new owners. I wonder if he hasn't already tried to poach some of yours now that Ivor's gone. Have you met all the owners in Ivor's. . . I mean your yard?"

Hassan and Whitey leaned over their dinner plates to listen carefully to my reply. Happy had left the dining room for the kitchen to serve the dessert. She didn't hear my answer.

"Thanks for asking, Lawrence. I've met four so far. Two earlier in the season, and two more today. All four were enchanted, really enchanted by Happy, too. But I'm not sure how they felt about me. After all, I didn't place for one, and came in second with the other owner's horse. Hassan, here, proved himself to be a clever trainer by beating our runner in the first fillies' race."

Hassan lowered his head in Muslim-taught modesty. I thought his expression was more like a teacher's pet pretending to be stupid.

After compliments to Happy for her dessert, Ellie suggested - in true British style - that the two ladies should leave the men to their brandies and cigars. Happy led Ellie upstairs to look in on Tim.

Ellie, despite still mourning Ivor, had helped arrange this dinner and attended it wearing her most fashionable celebrities' clothing. She wasn't looking for a lover to take Ivor's place. She genuinely wanted to help Happy and add her authentic British touches to the evening.

I served large snifters of my best brandy to Lawrence and Whitey, but Hassan - a Muslim - never drank alcohol and asked for orange juice.

I went into the kitchen to get it. Hassan followed me like a fox stalking a pheasant. He said, "My divine Sirena came with me to England. She's staying at the Dorchester. The hotel has a Muslim owner, you know, so I get a discount. I'll give you a night with her. Sex with her will send you into another universe."

"Hassan, thanks, but no thanks. I've told you: I love my wife."

"And all this domesticity? Baby howling upstairs, nanny under foot, worries about central heating? I tell you, it's another universe; sex you've never imagined." Hassan's faked Oxford accent became more pronounced. I thought he sounded like a debater in Parliament.

I tried to change the subject. "Ice with your orange juice?"

"Never take ice in my drinks, a habit from Dubai, where one might just pick up a deadly virus or worse. Rick, you're my friend and I want to do something memorable for you. I insist you spend a night with Sirena."

"Let's join the other guests," I said, trying to pluck him out of my kitchen like a man tries to rid himself of a disease-carrying tick.

Happy and Ellie had come downstairs. Ellie complained about the enveloping cigar smoke. She waved at it like a conductor using his baton. Happy just said, "Boys will be boys. My father smokes a corn cob pipe."

Whitey asked her, "Will you be meeting more of Ivor's owners during these next four days of Ascot? I heard from Rick that you've enchanted the one you've already met.

"Enchanted? Why, what a lovely thing to say! But I don't know about that. I've just been doing what any wife should do; be polite to the people who butter our bread."

Lawrence agreed with Whitey. "Yes, enchanted was what we heard. I wish I had a wife like you. Mine spends all her time watching TV sitcoms. Never the races, God, no. They might interfere with her finding out who's sleeping with whom."

"Is that why I haven't met her? I'd sure like to," Happy said politely, not pushing.

"She wouldn't even accompany me to England because she might miss an episode of her favorite programs. She doesn't give a damn about our owners or their horses. Leaves all the sucking up to me . . . and don't think I don't suck up to them. I've always thought keeping an owner is more important than winning races. If you lose an owner from your stable, you won't have a horse to run!"

Whitey interrupted, "You know, Rick, you should be entertaining your owners, not us trainers."

"Agreed. Happy and I are giving a lunch in the Turf Club tent on Thursday for three of my owners."

Hassan bulldozered back into the conversation: "I've never been in the Turf Club's tent; the club's main rooms in Central London, yes, but not the Royal Ascot tent."

"Then you must be my guest!" I laughed to myself, remembering that Be My Guest was the name of Diana Guest's great stallion. "Meet us at the tent on Thursday. Not drinking any alcohol, you'll be a cheap guest."

I wondered if Hassan often invited himself places.

Wednesday was a great day for Happy and me. First, my father came down from Warwickshire, to see his grandchild; he'd been pleased when we'd named our son after him. And, I suspect he wanted to check out if Tim looked like him!

Next, he accompanied us on the ride to the races.

We took a short cut to Ascot. We passed fields of golden rape, and brooks softened with the drooping sleeves of willows. A horse out to pasture gave a clue that we were approaching the town. We entered High Street to see new hanging baskets on lamp posts, and noticed that its distinguished tall clock had recently been repainted in the colors of Scotland's flag.

Further along loomed the enormous new grandstand. "Looks like an airport," Dad wheezed.

I was surprised by the changes made to the lawns leading to the grandstand: they had previously been very beautifully maintained, with white rails and stools around a pre-parade ring. That had been moved and now the lawns were separated into areas for club tents, general admission alleys, and champagne bars. There were *Versailles* boxes planted with white hydrangeas topped by pylons draped with ivy. There was a strip of an all-weather track to bring the competing horses in from beyond Car Park Number One. Along one side were the stools for spectators who wanted a good view before placing their bets.

I parked our car in the owners and trainers car park again, which meant crossing the High Street in front of the winding traffic of Bentleys and Rolls Royces heading for Car Park Number One. That car park was already nearly full, as longtime holders of their spaces were lunching out of the back of their cars. Picnic tables and grander terrace-type tables nestled under the trees where champagne and smoked salmon sandwiches were favorites. Some tables had floral centerpieces, and complete three-course menus accompanied by wines and spirits.

Thursday, Ladies Day, was very different. It started out with the threat of bad weather. That always meant that many women would opt out of coming to the races because they preferred to save their best clothes and hats for the indoor parties later on. Whatever the weather, my lunch was going to take place on schedule.

Crowds of Ladies Day partygoers streamed through the general admission gate. Many of the women wore outrageous costumes instead of suitable racing outfits: hats topped with intestine-looking decorations snaking up from their wide brims, three-feet-high feathers on some, and ankle-length dresses more suitable for ballroom dancing. These women might never look at a horse, much less watch a race. Their men wore no hats and their jackets were a sorry lot. Parallel to this river of partygoers came the more sedate members of the Royal Enclosure. Men in morning suits and top hats, favoring grey or black but no brown. Their ladies were discreetly outfitted in knee-length silks with matching hats, or hats that looked like parasols, their brims were so large.

The traditional gypsy flower vendors had been given the shove and were replaced by serious men selling blue cornflowers or carnations for buttonholes. Once through the security both crowds mingled and melded unlike in previous years when they'd been separated as neatly as the men and women at a Quaker meeting.

To the left of Car Park Number One's entrance gathered handsome carriages drawn there by smartly turned-out carriage horses, their tack glinting in the sunlight. It was fun watching the girls who'd chosen to come in these carriages as they tried to get down gracefully from their high perches without showing their knickers.

Happy couldn't resist going up to one of these heavy-footed horses and patting its soft nose.

With my trainer's badge I went into the enclosure more rapidly than Happy and Dad. While I waited for them to catch up with me, I stopped at one of the white wooden booths where official racecards were being sold, and bought one for each of them. They're good-looking programs with Her Majesty's crown and the E II boldly embossed on a cream-colored cover. I hurried to show Dad where my name was listed under trainers for the fifth race.

It was almost like swimming upriver against time to rejoin Dad and Happy, the crowds of people were pushing so hard to get to bars, boxes or hospitality tents.

Dad, seeming startled by the changes to his favorite racecourse, was blinking in the sunlight. He sounded hoarse when he spoke: "Rick, when the father of the present Viscount Churchill was HM's Representative at Royal Ascot, it was his job to weed out the people who were unsuitable for the Royal Enclosure. His method was simple. He categorized the wannabes as 'certainly', 'possibly', or 'certainly not'. Seems to me that this afternoon there's a strange mix of 'certainlys' with 'certainly nots'."

"Oh?" I didn't want to comment. I hoped Dad wasn't turning into a snob.

But now he chuckled deep in his throat and added, "Viscountess Churchill told me how an avalanche of dinner invitations would arrive for the two of them shortly before the date when applications were closed. Poor dears, they had to decline all invitations so as not to offend those they knew could not pass muster."

Bristling a little, and not because she had to hold tight to her hat to save it from cartwheeling off in the wind, Happy said, "I don't know what 'pass muster' means, but if folks who want to come racing can't, is it because they've been in prison?" For once I left Happy without the answer to a question. For all that she'd pored long hours over *Debrett's* and learned most of Britain's grander titles, I feared it wouldn't be possible to clarify the 'pass muster' expression in a few seconds standing in the wind at Royal Ascot.

Dad and Happy came into the pre-paddock and we walked with the filly's lad along the all-weather and under an overpass to reach the main paddock. We waited with other trainers with their owners while the fillies' lads marched them around the far side of the paddock until the stream of jockeys emerged to look for their owners and the trainers who had booked them through their agents for this race. My filly's owners had decided not to come to Royal Ascot. They'd had a hard time finding the money to enter the filly into this race and couldn't afford the day for themselves.

The "Jockeys please mount" call came. The time for last minute instructions to jockeys was over. Jockeys swung into saddles and gave one or more passes around the paddock either to steady their mounts or to show them to punters, and then it was under the overpass and through a short tunnel to emerge out onto the field. My filly balked at the tunnel. She hadn't seen anything like it before. But our jockey handled her well and pointed her to the starting gate. I wanted to go with a course executive by car to the gate to observe the filly's behavior there, but I hated to leave Happy, who so much longed to push her filly friend into her stall. I drew my binoculars from their case and ushered Dad and Happy to the Trainers' Stand.

"They're off!" The loudspeaker's commentator followed every inch of the race, his voice growing more excited as the fillies approached the final furlong. We could see what was happening perfectly thanks to a huge screen installed facing the stands. There was some pushing among the jockeys, not legal but carefully kept to the minimum permitted, and I was shocked to see one jockey's use of his whip which he'd soaked in water to give a cruel beating to his mount.

Our jockey took the far rail where the ground was marginally better, and softer on this sunny day. He didn't need to pull any nasty tricks.

It was a hard fought race.

And I won! Glorious!

I stood under the pole headed by a short sign reading 'First" and was surrounded by photographers and racing journalists. When will she run again? Sandown? Goodwood? Newmarket? I gave nothing away. The next race would depend on what the filly's owner wanted.

Happy looked charming and very British in a sensible silk suit with matching hat, selected, of course, by Ellie. Dear little Happy, she tried so hard to win over these three difficult owners and their snobbish wives. This time, however, she was less successful than she'd been at Beverley and Doncaster.

In the paddock, the first disaster came about when a gust of wind caught the huge hat worn by Lady Locke, my eldest owner's wife. The hat blew away and ended its career under a hoof of the Gold Cup favorite. With skills left over from her days as a girl jockey, Happy ran up to the horse and retrieved Lady Locke's hat - now crumpled and covered with manure. But she got a dirty look from the horse's owner, suggesting that Happy had pulled this as a trick in order to unsettle the favorite just before the race. Not true. She was just being a Baptist, you know, love thy neighbor; that was one of Happy's favorite sayings.

The Turf Club tent runs like the meals on an ocean liner. As we were scheduled to have the second seating, we had to gallop as fast as some of my no-hopers to get from the owners and trainers stand to the tent before our guests arrived.

Lord and Lady Locke snubbed our party and went to White's Tent instead. Mr. and Mrs. Hugh Gordon had showed up early and were looking peevish having to stand around while the first seating diners finished their meals, and our table was readied. Captain and Mrs. Ainsley arrived late. Flustered, Mrs. Ainsley had also suffered an accident with her hat and she looked as peevish as a housedog left out in the rain.

Worse, Hassan showed up with his unexpected and uninvited friend, Sirena. Our table had to be rearranged to accommodate an extra chair and place setting, causing the tent's staff to send angry glances in my direction.

"This is Sirena. You'll recall, Rick, I've wanted to introduce you two!"

Happy caught the nuances in his tone. Her antenna rose like the hackles on a tiger. She tried to seat Sirena across the table from me, but Sirena crowded in on my left. Very soon I felt her bare toes kneading my ankle. Then, slowly but expertly, her right hand worked its way from my knee to my groin. Unwelcome desire shot through me like pellets from a shotgun.

Her fingers played, tantalizingly, working their way to my crotch. Bingo! I 'came' there and then, ruining my Ascot pants, and right in front of my most important owners.

Splash! Happy overturned her glass of orange juice sending the contents swirling across the table and on to Sirena's couture chiffon dress. Sirena's outfit couldn't really even be referred to as a dress; it was more like a babydoll nightgown - silky, transparent, and low-cut at the neckline while hanging high up above her shapely knees.

"Oh! So sorry," Happy purred. "Let me take you to the ladies' room and sponge off the orange juice."

Clever professional that she was, Sirena made no fuss. She dabbed at the silk, pulling the skirt higher, and followed Happy to the ladies' room like a puppy out for a stroll on a leash.

The ladies' room was located outside the Turf Club in a narrow alleyway, with steep steps leading up into its small interior. Sirena tripped on the steps, skinned her knee and tore the hem of her skimpy dress. Again, she made no complaint. She went to the toilet for a very long session, as though she had other needs beyond the expected. Happy waited patiently, like a governess with an unruly child. She said a few words to Sirena that actually made that pro blush.

When they returned to the table, Sirena bypassed me to turn her eyes, like a pair of powerful floodlights, on my richest British owner, Hugh Gordon, who was seated to her left.

For fun, and I suppose curiosity, I watched as Sirena repeated the same maneuvers on him that she'd played earlier on me. First the bare footsie, then the hand climbing his thigh to the important bits.

His wife had been watching closely, but not out of curiosity. With an unladylike roar, turning heads in our direction from every table in the club, she grabbed her husband's morning coat by one shoulder and physically dragged him outside. No "goodbye, and thank you for lunch," either.

"My God," I groaned. "I hope I haven't lost Hugh Gordon as an owner."

Hassan, trying to mask a smug expression, chortled, "Let's all go to The Dorchester for dinner. My treat!"

Captain Ainsley, known as one who never refuses a free meal, accepted with alacrity, although his wife was wearing a wary look. Since I had no runners the next day, I agreed to go to The Dorchester as well. By the time we finished our lunch, it was teatime, and the club needed our table. We rushed to the car park to leave for London before the tidal wave of Ladies Day parents with debutante daughters erupted through the exits.

With cell phones not permitted on the course to prevent illegal betting, Happy had to wait until we got to the car park. She dialed home. " Mrs. Roe has taken off to see her sick sister. She's left Tim with Ellie. You know I think the world of Ellie, but alone with Tim? I think I'd better go on home!" Happy wailed.

Captain Ainsley overheard and suggested in a kind voice, "Take your family car, Mrs. Harrow. I'll drive Rick to The Dorchester, and take him home later. It's not too far out of my way."

Happy was suffering from a mental tug-of-war: should she stay and protect me from Sirena, or rush to her baby's bedside? She chose Tim.

She said, in her new-found elocution, "Rick, my darling, you'll be fine in Captain Ainsley's capable hands. I'll kiss Tim good night for you."

I didn't know it yet but I wasn't safe from Sirena. When we arrived at The Dorchester and Captain Ainsley's wife called their home to check on their dogs, she wailed, "Bruno's got a terrible itch. Mange! We've got to rush him to a vet this instant." The Ainsleys drove away without even a goodbye, or thanks for lunch. Again, I wondered, would I lose them as owners?

Oiling his way into the deserted dining room, Hassan called over the *maitre d'* and demanded a quiet table in a corner. I looked up at the wall murals and wished I could disappear into one of them.

In my bones, I felt Hassan would invent an excuse to leave me alone with Sirena. He did. Within minutes, he said an owner in California was expecting his call, and with the eight hour time difference it was the ideal time for him to call her. "Cheaper to call by my mobile than to use the hotel phones," was his excuse. Cell phone in hand, he disappeared.

A courtly old-time waiter brought us large menu cards and draped pristine napkins over our laps. Very soon, I felt Sirena's fingernails scratching in a provocative way as her right hand worked up high toward my nether parts. Her bare toes did their work under the table.

Suddenly she stretched out her hand to grab my hand - the one not holding the menu. In her sultry sex-offering voice she started working me. Looking at my palm, she suggested that she could tell my fortune. With one fingernail acting like a scout she traced the battlefield of my life line.

I ruined my striped pants for the second time that day,and hoped the hotel's napkin hadn't been soaked in semen, too.

Sirena lowered her voice to a contralto. "Let's go upstairs. We can order here and have our food sent up to my room . . ."

"No! Tell Hassan I'm skipping dinner. Happy may need me to go get food for my baby son. There's no nanny at home."

I didn't even say goodbye, or a thank you. That sort of behavior seemed to have gone out of fashion.

Striding out of the restaurant like a man called to the bedside of his dying parent, I hailed a cab. Would I have enough money on me to pay the fare? I didn't give a damn. I asked to be taken to the railroad station, where I could get my ticket with a credit card, and hoped my small store of cash would take care of the ticking meter's final sum. It did. I caught the last train to Epsom and spent most of the time in the men's room. I threw away my underpants and sponged the crotch of my trousers. I figured it wouldn't matter if they were wet, as long as they were clean. I could tell Happy I'd spilled water on myself while pouring it to mix with my whiskey at The Dorchester.

Ellie met me at the Epsom station. "Tim's fine," she reassured me. "Asleep now. Your wife's with him. She's waiting for you."

At home Happy warned me not to wake Tim, said she'd already given him a goodnight kiss for me. She ushered Ellie out the front door with repeated thanks, and when we went upstairs to our bedroom she sank into my arms with such passion that once again I felt glad that Baptists believe in lovemaking.

9

We stayed home Friday, and skipped Royal Ascot. I had no runners for Friday's very special races.

Instead, a pile of bills and questions from owners waited for me. But first thing first; I went down to the stables to oversee the horses for early morning gallops.

Happy went with me, leaving Tim with a repentant Mrs. Roe. "What are your owners whining about?"

"The usual. They want to know why their colts aren't winning races. But among our best-lookers, with perfect conformation, bursting with health, and shining coats there's a crib-biter, a sex-crazy three-year-old, and one who won't even try to win a race."

Happy didn't raise her eyebrows at 'sex-crazy.' No snide looks either. Snide simply doesn't apply where Happy's concerned. She said, "Tell me more."

I led her to the crib-biter's stall. His expensive door was badly nibbled along the top edge. "His name's on the plate. BillandBea, owned by William and Beatrice. They're cheapos, and give me just enough money for basics."

"No carrots? No apples?" Happy dug into a bag full of apples and offered one to the colt. He stared at it, curious. Finally, he took a nibble. His eyes lit up, and he stared at the rest. Happy produced another. He mouthed that one in an instant and nudged Happy's hand for more. She whispered in his ear, and gave him one last morsel.

"What did you tell him?" I knew from our days in Kentucky that Happy had a special way of communicating with horses. I remembered her success with terrible Attila.

"I told him he'd get a belly-ache if he ate any more apples today, but if he wins his race tomorrow, I'll give him more."

We moved on to the sex-crazy colt's stall. We could hear him before we saw him. He was neighing like the sirens for an air raid.

His powerful hooves were beating on the floor, sending straw flying. In the straw's dust, he snorted as noisily as a locomotive.

I said, "Happy, don't get too close to him. He wasn't named So-And-So for nothing. There won't be much you can do for this boy."

"That's what *you* think. Go make your mornin' rounds. We have some talkin' to do. He likes mares in season."

"Careful, darling. You're the most precious person in the world to me."

I sneaked a look back into So-And-So's stall door to reassure myself that Happy was safe; she was staring into his eyes and he was perfectly still.

I finished my rounds and asked Happy how she was getting on with So-And-So. I didn't need to ask; I could see he felt calm, and yet his ears were pricked.

"We're getting along just fine!"

"So I see. And what miracle did you pull off this time?"

"I simply told him if he didn't win a race he'd end up as dog food. But if he won some good ones he'd be syndicated as

70

a stallion, and be given forty mares a year for the rest of his life."

I laughed so hard I was afraid I'd split my well-worn cords. I patted So-And-So's neck, and we moved on to my last difficult colt. "His name's Lonelyheart. So, Happy, are you going to have a conversation with him, too?"

"I don't need to. I read his passport in your office. This colt's from Arkansas. He's homesick, wants American oats and grass. Send him to Whitey. I'll bet he could win the Arkansas Derby."

"Nice thought, my darling wife. But I can't afford to lose any horses." I dug my cold hands into my cords's pockets. "His owner won't spend the shipping costs to fly him over to Arkansas. That's expensive. And I don't have the cash to buy him and ship him myself. Anyway, I can't antagonize his owner. He's part of my future here."

"Offer Whitey to trade. He could have a good colt, but with sore hooves, who could run better on English grass instead of hard American turf. Make it a clean trade. Your owner could be delighted by Whitey's horse. It's better than one that won't try."

Gratefully I returned to my well-heated office. I telephoned Whitey with my offer to trade Lonelyheart. He lunged at the idea, and knew of a horse in his stable with sore hooves, named Feathers. He was sure his owner would offer to pay transport for both horses. We made a date to have lunch again in the Turf Club on the last day of Royal Ascot.

I settled at my desk to face the near-impossible task of paying my stable's mounting bills. As it turned out, Ivor's estate was debt-ridden. He hadn't owned the house where he'd killed himself. He leased the stables and gallops from one of his owners. We sorely needed to win some races.

I love the final day of Royal Ascot. It's usually very relaxed, with most of Saturday's racegoers serious about horse flesh. The snobs opted to go to their country places, taking their debutante daughters with them. And office workers who'd been tied to their desks from Monday through Friday could at last enjoy the wonders of Ascot, their faces alight with pleasure, not like those dulled by blasé sophistication.

In 2006 children from ten to sixteen could come to the racecourse all five days at a reduced price. In 2003 Ascot launched the Colts & Fillies Club for its younger racegoers. It's free to the kids, and they get a special club badge to wear during Family Days along with a horse racing activity book, puzzles and a game. During the year they receive a regular newsletter with updates from the club mascot, Scotty, and cards on their birthdays. There's a barbeque that parents can attend, but only if accompanied by a child.

Happy was pleased that Ascot offers a center for young mothers to leave their infants, safely supervised, for up to two hours - supposedly enough time for a meal and a to watch a race or two.

"I don't know if your owners will finish their lunches in two hours, so I'll have to leave you and go to Tim," Happy commented.

Our Saturday lunch started out with trouble brewing.

Hugh Gordon had telephoned with an excuse, and added he was taking his horses away from me and sending them to Hassan.

Captain Ainsley insisted I join him in Car Park Number One, which had a long walk before reaching the newly placed premier enclosure for members. Mrs. Ainsley's high heels kept getting caught in the grass, and finally one heel broke off and sent her to her knees. Captain Ainsley said, "I'm beginning to wonder, Rick, if you're bad luck for me. First my dog gets mange, and now my wife has had a fall." He stalked off to his own club's tent, helping his wife limp along, and left me stuck to pay for two empty seats at our table.

Happy proceeded to do what she could to mend fences. She chased after Mrs. Ainsley and offered to trade shoes. Mrs. Ainsley accepted with some grace, and then it was Happy's turn to limp around Ascot's Royal Enclosure, missing a heel on one of her traded shoes. She limped into Ascot's shop and bought a small box of get well cards and limped over to the Ainsley's club's tent to deliver a card for their ailing dog.

Ascot's new parade ring is situated behind the grandstand on its south side. The architect designed it to be the heart of the racecourse. The weighing room is at its top, which means jockeys who win a race won't forget to weigh in. We were standing in the pre-parade ring, some meters away from the saddling boxes, when Happy whispered, "Rick darling, don't worry about losing Hugh as an owner. I've just seen his wife looking like a rattlesnake sizing up a toad, when Hugh walked by arm-in-arm with Sirena. Hugh will be delivered back on our doorstep in no time by his wife. I guarantee it."

I followed her glance. Happy was right. If Hugh had been more alert, he'd have heard the rattles.

Sirena smiled, glowingly like a world champion standing on the winner's platform. I might have wet my trousers, but I didn't; I had work to do. I joined my head lad at the saddling boxes and located our slot. With satisfaction I noted that our colt was the best turned-out, and was duly named as such over the microphone. We walked him from the pre-parade ring through a tunnel to the paddock. He was acting somewhat skittish due to the traffic noise from Ascot High Street not many meters beyond.

Happy settled him by whispering into his ear. Jockeys swirled into the parade ring, their silks glinting in the various colors of their owners, and searched out their mounts. Our head lad, Tom, gave our jockey a leg up. He circled the parade ring, walked under a second tunnel and was away, cantering down the field to show the betting public his action.

I led Happy to the owners and trainers stand, to see if I recognized any old friends. There were none. A big turnover in trainers had taken place here during the years I'd spent in the U.S.

In 2004, I'd brought Arrow to Royal Ascot. He'd won his race. Then the top owners on the flat were Godolphin, Hamdam Al Maktoum, the Cheveley Park stud, Ballymacoll Stud, K.Abdullah, Sheik Mohammed, my friend the Duke of Roxburghe, and of course, H.H. the Aga Khan. None of those names appeared on Ivor's list.

A longtime friend entered the stand late. It was Paul Cole. He winked at me, apparently glad to see I was back in Britain. I guess that also might mean he felt no rivalry, because he didn't think I'd inherited any horses from Ivor that could compete with his owners' horses.

Paul was a trainer at the Elite Racing Club. The Club's concept was simple: members pay an affordable twelve months subscription; they share in the fun and excitement of following the careers of the club's twenty racehorses; best of all, they share in equal parts the prize money won by the horses. For the club, Paul trained Brecon Beacon, Eissteddfod and Oceans Apart. The club has had over two hundred winning races. Members also share the club's racing colors: an all-white jacket with three large black spots placed diagonally, and a black cap. The club's president is my longtime nemesis, the racing commentator Lord Oaksey, who always seemed to demean my string.

Surprise! Our crib-biter won the race. And Happy was right there with his apples as he went into the parade ring to stand under the pole proclaiming 'First.'

Being owners in my stable, Captain and Mrs. Ainsley crowded into the parade ring. But the crib-biter's owner never appeared. He'd waived spending the expense of coming to Royal Ascot, confident that poor miserable BillandBea could never pass the finish line first.

This was the same race I'd won two years ago when the fake Baroness had gone into such a rage for not having met The Queen or having a trophy given to her from the gloved regal hands on the dais.

My roller coaster luck went into a dive again after that race. Hassan showed up with Sirena, crowing about his new owner, Hugh.

With children skipping around us it was difficult to put on a furious face. I liked the fact that children are allowed at Ascot. Some of the boys have full morning coats and striped trousers accompanied by tall silk hats. Little girls wear their party dresses and fly over the grass like butterflies in a mating season. Lovely!

Uncharacteristically, it was Happy who gave Hassan and Sirena a put-down. In a very distinct tone, recently acquired from her elocution lessons, she snapped: "Something smells very bad here, and it isn't the horse manure. I suspect it's you, Sirena. Or you, Hassan."

Abashed, Sirena and Hassan scuttled away.

Loyal little Happy continued to limp over to the pre-parade ring to watch our last runner, Anchor, be saddled. Then, she limped into the parade ring and over to the trainers and owners stand.

But her trade of shoes with Mrs. Ainsley paid off. The Ainsleys trailed us up to the paddock, and when our runner won, they went right up on the dais with us for HM The Queen's presentation of a trophy.

Anchor's absent owner had delegated me to receive any trophies his horse might win. My glory moment arrived on that dais, with Happy by my side. The Queen gave me a rare compliment: "Well done, Harrow."

I made a cavalry officer's deep head-bent-low bow, and said, "Ma'am, may I present my wife, Hillary?" I didn't dare use her nickname in the sovereign's presence.

The Queen gave her a smile that was like sunshine coming out from parting clouds. She murmured, "I see you are expecting a baby. When is it due?"

"Oh!" Happy could barely squeak out one word. "October."

Our knowledgeable racehorse-owning Queen stated, "I hope that doesn't mean you'll miss our Ascot Festival in September."

HM The Queen turned her head to hint that Happy's moment was over, as she swiveled toward our jockey with congratulations and astute comments on his ride.

All I could think of was that I'd made Ivor proud. Happy put that nicely for the racing correspondents who pushed around us once we'd left the dais. She said, using her elocution lessons to the fullest, "Rick gives all the credit for the wins today to Ivor Wren, who bought the horses as yearlings and did most of their preparation."

Good wife. She said the correct thing. No slang, no calling these glorious wins "a double."

When the reporters left us to interview the owner of the final race on Ascot's newly renovated flat and jump courses, Happy rested her cheek on my shoulder and returned to her old Kentucky accent. "Ah'm in heaven, darlin'! Ah met the Queen and she even asked me about our comin' baby. Wow!"

Happy had more scintillating first-timers that day. Cameras popped their flashes at her, and the popular racing commentator Miss Clare Balding interviewed her about the second-hand 'celebrity' dress and hat she wore, prodding to know the name of the resale shop.

The Ainsleys managed to get in the photograph taken by the racing press. Not with HM, but with us and Anchor. From their smiles I could gauge that Captain Ainsley no longer thought I was a bad-luck trainer.

I remembered that the Captain was known never to refuse a free meal.But he surprised me by offering to help us celebrate in the Royal Enclosure premier admission area, and he paid for the champagne.

Later, after we'd downed the contents of our flutes of champagne, and Happy her orange juice, she limped all the way back to Car Park Number One to return Mrs.Ainsley's broken shoes. That was the deciding factor that endeared us to the Ainsleys. Carrying the half-full bottle of champagne which he put into his car's bar, the Captain said, "I'll be down for early morning gallops tomorrow, Rick old chap!"

I felt as buoyant as a kid wearing rubber swimming wings as I received nods of congratulations all the way to the trainers' car park.

Suddenly, my imaginary swimming wings deflated at the sight of poor Whitey. He'd come all the way from Arkansas with his string and hadn't won a race all week. He looked as downtrodden as a bug underfoot.

Lawrence was trying to cheer him by shaking a container of martinis. Lawrence said, "My horses didn't win anything either. Expensive experiment, bringing them here. I should have saved them for Arlington. Chicago's so much closer."

He couldn't crack a smile from Whitey. His face was as tight as the blocks of a cement sidewalk.

Happy felt like jumping, she wanted me to know she was really back in her own two good shoes. She jumped up, and wound her arms around Whitey. "Cheer up, shuga', you're goin' to have a wonderful horse to take home with you. I tell you, he'll win the Arkansas Derby. He's called Lonelyheart, and we'll trade him for one of your runners that would do better on soft English grass."

Whitey and I discussed the particulars of the trade, and how we could convince the owners.

Feeling somewhat deflated after the day's excitement, I drove Happy home. My satisfaction returned like wind into the sails of a schooner when we watched the nine o'clock news replaying of our races, and the presentation of Anchor's trophy by HM.

Best of all was the sex when we went to bed that night. Glorious.

10

I thought, 'Maybe we had too much sex and it affected Happy's pregnancy.' She began to have dizzy spells, couldn't keep her food down, and she lost her concentration.

Though she'd proved invaluable in the stables with the horses, and in my office with the books, our new baby came first. So, I decided to hire an assistant trainer.

After interviewing a half-dozen hopefuls who either couldn't work a computer, or didn't know a horse's withers from his ass, I settled on a thirty-year-old from Newcastle, named Burp Trent. Nice boy, except for an annoying habit of prefacing all his remarks with "Crist-on-a-bike." Annoying!

"I'm from chapel folk," he told me first thing. I knew *that* would please Happy. "I'm my parents' sixth child, they'd had five girls before I was born. I arrived on Bank Holiday Monday, which is why I'm nicknamed Burp. My Mum had the burps from drinking all that day." He finally drew breath, but only to change the subject. "I live for horses. All I've ever done was clean out stables and yards, or ride early morning gallops. I can't bring any new owners into our yard but I'll do my damnedest to give you everything else you need."

He did try hard. Burp wasn't God's gift to horseracing, but little-by-little he learned the more complicated skills necessary to turn a no-hoper into a winner.

Burp liked to talk, non-stop. I had entered a no-hoper into a small race up North in Pontrefact, and took Burp with me to help with the saddling-up. I figured he was familiar with the area and the local customs.

It's a five hour drive from my yard to the Pontrefact racecourse. We left on a perfect July morning, passing villages of thatched roofed houses, with some roofs cut into fanciful forms. One village had Morris dancers performing on its town green; the bells on their white socks which jingled merrily.

Burp had comments for everything. "Crist-on-a-bike, in my village we've had jugglers ever since the Middle Ages. One even juggles in front of statues at the Catholic church!"

I decided to shift the subject matter to horse racing. I said, "Pontrefact isn't totally unknown territory for me. My father won a race here in the 1970s, and as a kid he brought me along. He had a good filly at the time, called La Valeuse."

Burp interrupted to show off his knowledge of French: "The thief."

"Right you are. And she stole the race from a filly belonging to Viscountess Rothermere. The true story is that, following the race, Lady Rothermere *gave* her filly to my father. I imagine she thought close proximity to the winner might improve her filly to the point where she could win a race. Mary Rothermere was from Texas, born a Murchison, she truly loved her horses."

"Nice story. Crist-on-a-bike, do you know any more?"

I smiled. But my eyebrows twitched and I felt like a warning light had been switched on when a plane enters turbulence. I didn't want to share my racing stories with anyone other than Happy.

Though Burp, like a terrier tugging at a trouser cuff, kept at me. "Just one more!"

"Well, I do know another story about an owner who so loved her horse that she gave her away. This one involves my fellow cavalry officer, an Eleventh Hussar, Tim Foster, and winner of the 1971 Grand National."

"Over the jumps, not the flat?"

"Right you are again. The story goes like this. An elderly lady in delicate health, who had always yearned to win the Grand National, recognized a particular horse's potential. The horse's trainer was Tim Foster, in whom she had complete confidence. When this dear lady's health declined to the point she was about to die, she signed all the necessary papers to transfer ownership of that horse to Tim. And, shortly after her death, the horse won the Grand National."

"Beautiful!"

"Yes, and Tim came right up into the stands afterwards to have a word with my father. He said, 'Tim, you've never wanted to have a jump horse before. How about owning this one with me, now that I've won the Grand National.' Since he was named Tim, and my father was Tim, Foster obviously had thought that would be enough to convince my father to train with him."

"And did he?"

"No. My father had run out of money by that time and didn't want to sell any more land to buy any more racehorses."

Pontrefact proved lucky for me that day. I bought Burp lunch. He gloried in the local smoked eels, and then we walked in a leisurely way down to the paddock. Burp was quite capable to saddle up the runner but I helped him, not wanting to take any chances with a loose belt.

My runner that day belonged to Captain Ainsley, who hadn't believed his no-hoper could do anything other than eat. He hadn't even wanted to pay for the gas all the way to Pontrefact just to watch him come in Fourth, or worse. He'd decided to give the race a pass. Too bad, he'd have been overjoyed seeing him come in first.

After the win, we were invited into the Directors' Room for drinks. Burp was ecstatic. He kept repeating his favorite Newcastle expression: "Crist-on-a-bike!" He'd climbed up the ladder of racing society faster than he could ever have imagined - all in one day.

All the way back to Epsom, he offered racing stories he knew from history books. He began with King Charles II and the royal mistresses and bastards. "The king established the cradle of English racing at Newmarket, with rules and traditions. That doesn't mean, as you well know, that there wasn't any serious racing in England before that. The Romans competed with their chariot horses. Elizabeth I encouraged her warriors to fight the Spanish on a ground used for racing. But, Crist-on-a-bike, of all Britain's monarchs, I like naughty King Charles the best. He had such amazing mistresses, the French one he made Duchess of . . . what was it . . . de Keroualle. And 'the protestant whore,' as Nell Gwynne called herself, who gave him the bastards he named Duke of Richmond, and the Earl of St. Albans. In fact, we might be going racing soon at Goodwood, which was carved out of the estate of the Duke of Richmond."

"Right again. We will be going to Goodwood. That course is just about perfect for Anchor. And I might put BillandBea in the big sprint for the Stewards' Cup."

Then, Burp did some more verbal sprinting. "My favorite, among the past royals who raced, was King Ted. He had plenty of mistresses too. Most of his mistresses were as knowledgeable about horses as he was. He took Daisy Brooke to all the fashionable courses the first time in history that a Prince of Wales or a King took his mistress to the races. She was a society lady accustomed only to society events. After Daisy, he took Lily Langtry, the daughter of the Dean of Jersey, to race meetings whenever he pleased. She thanked him by lending him money for horses when he thought he was financially strapped. And, there was Mrs. Keppel, by whom he may have had a daughter. Naturally, I'm not comparing him to our present Prince of Wales, although it's a known fact that the new Duchess of Cornwall's great-grandmother was, shall we say, intimate with Edward VII. In fact, correct me if I'm wrong, but I believe I read that Edward VII was so fond of Mrs. Keppel that his Queen, Alexandra of Denmark, invited her to his bedside when the king was dying."

I meditated on that. Would my Happy invite Sirena to my bedside? I was jolly sure she wouldn't. Our home was no Buckingham Palace, but I felt that even our humble cottage would never be open to the likes of Sirena.

Wrong again! Pulling into the short drive that led to my cottage I recognized Hassan's ostentatious Daimler. My front door was opened by Sirena.

From the stairs I heard Happy's voice calling to me in her perfect elocution lessons voice, "Darling we've been invited to Dubai for the big race. And I've said we'll go."

11

Why had Happy agreed to Sirena's invitation, delivered from Hassan? I knew I'd have to wait until we had our two heads on our pillows to get her reason. I'd watched her devour all the racing news from Dubai. She was fascinated how Electrocutionist had won the World Cup's $3.6 million purse for the UAR's Sheik Mohammed. She was worried that Electrocutionist would be a strong contender to beat when Simon Crisford, Godolphin's racing manager, announced: "He ran very much in the mould of Swain and we'll take a similar route with him, including the Coronation Cup and King George at Ascot, and then to America for the Breeders' Cup." Not good news for our stable because I'd entered our best horses all in the same races.

Meanwhile I had to play the hospitable host, and go see if I had on ice the martini mix Sirena liked.

I followed her into my cottage which was permeated with the scent of her oriental perfume. *My manhood hardened.* I headed for the kitchen, but my eyes followed Sirena. She'd entered the drawing room. There, on the floor, was my father, lying horizontal, playing with baby Tim. They were using building blocks to create a tower. Sirena joined them. She lay down on the floor also horizontal, but she opened her knees and then stretched out her arms to invite Tim to be cradled by her. Watching her, I almost bumped into the kitchen door.

Tailing behind me came Burp, also fascinated by the scene on the drawing room floor. He said, "That's your Dad, isn't it? He seems very happy with his new wife."

Sirena, my father's wife! What gave him that idea? And then I saw what prompted Burp to suggest my eighty-year-old father had married Sirena. The fly on his pants was open. Sirena cradled my son with one arm, while her free hand played with my father's manhood.

I coughed, announcing my entry to the drawing room. Father sat up with a radiant expression. He zipped his pants, behaving like a teenager caught "borrowing" the family's car. His expression told us: Not a criminal offense, just having some fun.

Burp came in suddenly. "Something's burning in the kitchen. What shall I do?"

Happy wailed from upstairs. "I smell my potatoes burning and that's all I had to serve with the roast."

I thought, "Yes, and something's burning in the drawing room, too."

Sirena sat up quickly, and called to Happy, "Do you have any rice in the house? Raisins? Shredded coconut?"

No trace of embarrassment from her.

Happy trundled down the stairs. She'd lost her graceful model-like walk and figure. Her pregnancy had come into full bloom. She had a bump sticking out like the prow of a yacht. She walked more like a jockey now than when she'd *been* a jockey - her legs rounded from the extra weight. "I sure do. Rice, raisins, coconut bits."

She led Sirena into the kitchen. Sirena took a dishtowel and wrapped it over her $1000 dress. Sirena took a bottle of olive oil and proceeded to create a dish of middle-eastern rice. It was served with Happy's roast in our miniscule dinette.

Delicious!

Sirena acted like a changed woman. Totally domestic. She helped heap the rice on our plates. After we'd eaten, she took the dirty dishes to the sink and washed them. What was this all about?

My father hadn't a clue there was anything strange going on. From his Sirena experience, he was in what Happy used to call 'hog heaven' before elocution lessons. He behaved like a bridegroom at his bachelor party. All evening, the grin never left his face. I thought, 'All these years I believed my father hated the idea of remarriage, and rejected all women after my mother died in childbirth. Maybe what he really wanted all along was love and sex, like most other men.'

I felt guilty that perhaps I'd failed him as a son.

The evening grew long, but no one seemed eager to leave. Burp was as bowled over by Sirena as my father had been.

Sirena ended the evening by suggesting, "Why don't I give your father a lift back to Warwickshire."

"No! No way!" I gargled. I could imagine what two hours alone with Sirena on a back seat in a chauffeur driven limousine would do to Dad. At the very least, he could have a stroke.

I said, "Mrs. Roe's away visiting her sister for a week. Dad can sleep in her bedroom."

Happy, as ever my loyal back-up, chirped, "Come along, Dad. I'll change the sheets and give you an extra blanket. Burp, you can show Sirena to her car."

I didn't initiate sex that night, figuring that Dad would hear our gasps and yelps.

Happy wanted a story instead. First, I wanted her to explain why Sirena had been admitted into our home.

"Easy. Sirena appeared at the door with the invitation to Dubai."

"And?"

"She told me how much money you'd make if you won. Enough to pay off the yard debts, and for Tim's school fees for three years. He'll be in a nursery within twenty months, and the good ones are so expensive."

No contest. We could barely afford Mrs. Roe. And if I lost owners? We needed the money. I changed the subject. "I'll tell you a little about superstitions around racetracks. Luck! It's all important. But I'll tell you about it in Alfred Gwynn Vanderbilt's own words that he wrote in his book, *Horse and Horsemen*.:

> 'We had a big year last year. This year would be even better. Why not? We had more horses than anyone else. We had good help, good riders, good feed, good equipment, good this and good that. We looked like a 'cinch' to lead the list again. In the middle of May, we moved to Belmont. Good harvest managed to win the Metropolitan in what was a very roughly run race. We were in luck....Then one day I got a letter from a man in Canada. The writing was odd and the language worse. It read:
>
> > Although I am a stranger to you I am asking you to do me a favor..I have a system how to beat the mutual machines. It's a vision system, in other words, a Godsent. It takes $2,500 to work the system, you never lose a race, and you

don't have to play every horse in every race. It's a five horse system in every race. And it's guarantee $3,000 to $5,000 each day...I have written a few letters to different people and this is what happens to them for not answering my letters: J.K.L.Ross of Montreal and he went broke within two years ...Another letter went to H.P.Whitney in care of trainer Rowe... Mr. Whitney died three weeks after he received my letter and his trainer died a few months late... A letter also wasn't answered by Jockey Westrope when he was the leading jockey of America; bad luck will always follow him. So, remember, Mr. Vanderbilt, I have the right to give you back the $2,500 if I wish ..I will pray for you to send me the money by the 30th of May.'"

Happy interrupted to ask, "And did Mr. Vanderbilt send him the money?"

"No. He was also asked to send the Canuck seven shirts. He didn't do that either. Let me tell you more of what Vanderbilt wrote:

'We laughed about it...And promptly forgot about it. On the 30th of May we expected a big day. cherry Orchard was in the first race; she had trained nicely. she stumbled and fell at the break and our jockey, Johnny Bejshak, got a broken collar-bone. That necessitated a change of jockeys on Airflame as Johnny had always ridden him. I put Sammy Renick up,and saw him go down to defeat for the first time. I put Jackie

Westrope on Identify with orders to force the pace as strongly as possible. Westrope and Identify did their job well, but when the real issue came the red and white colors were not there. It had been a bad day. We still forgot the crank from Canada, for every stable has a bad day. We had a boy called McCombs who was making a name for himself as a rider. But when McCombs was thrown from a horse called Bristle, suffering an injured knee which laid him up for three months, we thought our luck was not so good. Maybe this Canuck crank knew what he was talking about.'"

"Poor jockeys!" Happy moaned.
"There's more:

'Discovery was training superbly. Skinny Fallon was being groomed to ride him while Bejshak recuperated. Meanwhile, we took Airflame to Suffolk Downs and broke the track record. We couldn't complain. So when Airflame showed a slight indication one morning to favor one of his hind legs, we decided: we have all these nice big two-year-olds we have saved expressly for the big money in Saratoga, let's let Airflame grow and rest on the farm. Then we got the cough. It went through the barn from end to end, putting us pretty well out of commission just when we really expected to go to town. Saratoga opened and instead of having everything to run we had pretty nearly nothing. We picked up the Saratoga Handicap with Discovery, but in it Good Gamble pulled up sore and Skinny Fallon, who rode her, was sent down for rough riding. Good Harvest had trained off after winning the Metropolitan Handicap and was just beginning to come back. One morning we were working him a mile and he bolted through the fence, running a piece of it through his chest and out the back of the saddle. Sammy Renick was thrown and shaken up but not seriously hurt. Now Discovery has one peculiarity; he has won time and time again for small purses, but every time we had him lined up to go for really big money something has happened to beat him. Either he has not run his race or been badly fouled, or he's been too highly weighted. In the Special, he broke last and ran for five furlongs; a bad last. Then he started to move, mowing down the leaders in a burst of speed that was amazing - even to me. He caught Time Supply and moved to Rosemont, so close to him, however, Rosemont's jockey accidentally struck him in his face as they reached the wire causing him to flinch at the crucial moment. The race went to Rosemont with Discovery second... Discovery ran a terrible race back of Roman Soldier in the Havre de Grace Handicap, and disclosed after the race the cause of most of his bad races - he hit his hocks and refused to extend himself. We sent him to the farm and advertised him for the stud next spring. It's funny about superstitions. I suppose some people would have taken the Canuck letter seriously and sent him $2,500 and seven old shirts, and let him bet on five or six horses in every race and make himself a fortune. Of course you know and I know that a shirt in Canada doesn't affect a horse in Maryland, or make Discovery hit his hocks or break Bejshak's collar-bone or kill Good Harvest... Still I wonder if that wouldn't have been $2,500 well spent.'"

"So ended Mr. Vanderbilt's comments on luck."

Happy sighed. "Just shows how hard it can be to win. And how easy to lose races. Enough talk. Give me one of your deep kisses."

I did. We had another memorable night, even though Dad could hear us.

Dad left for Warwickshire before early morning gallops. He still wore a radiant expression. I'd have loved to have shown him Anchor being trained for the Cup and So-And-So who, if he won, could have a career covering mares.

Now we had additional work to do. Whitey had quickly flown a fine looking two-year-old to England in exchange for Lonelyheart. I figured that by next season he could be an Epsom Derby prospect. There was so much I liked about the colt, including his name, Feathers. We kept that as a nickname, but his UK name was Feathermelightly.

I could have run him on our home course, right there at Epsom, but being a bit superstitious myself, I chose a small race for him at Lingfield - believed to be the ideal course for proving future Derby prospects. Also, I got a kitten to keep Feathers company in his stall. Whitey had told me that Feathers liked to have an animal friend to sleep with him on his straw. The kitten's name is Bumbles, and she loves Feathers just as much as Feathers loves her.

We brought Bumbles along to Lingfield - a cozy old-fashioned track where a visiting kitten would be equally welcome.

On the road to Lingfield, I talked to Burp about Saratoga and promised to take him there with us if Happy and I traveled there with the horses from Ivor's yard. "Beautiful old trees, friendly staff, great breakfasts for us after early morning gallops. And the owners are cordial. I remember meeting George Widener, one of the great old men of racing, and also an important collector in the world of art. There's a wing in the Philadelphia Museum named for him, as well there should be. Even at his advanced age, I thought he was one of the handsomest Americans I'd ever seen: straight back, elegant nose, kindly eyes. And yet I've met others of the Widener clan who don't measure up in the looks department. One, in particular, makes me think of the children's story where a princess kisses a frog and he turns into a prince, only, in reverse! This guy looks as though he'd been a prince who got the wrong kiss and turned into a frog."

Arriving at Lingfield, and loving the sight of its welcoming old buildings, I received a shock. I was summoned to the Directors' Room, where I learned bad news.

"Sorry to have to relay this to you," the Clerk of the Course said gloomily, "but your wife just called to let you know Colin Whitey died last night in Arkansas. It was sudden. Appears he had a heart attack."

I nodded and said nothing, my stomach was churning. Whitey? A heart attack? He'd looked so well during Royal Ascot. He couldn't have been older than thirty-five, and was a totally fit sportsman who skied, paddled rapids, and swam long distances.

Some niggling doubts wormed their way into my brain about this news. Had Whitey been murdered and his death made to look like natural causes? And if so, why? Who would want to murder Whitey?

I resolved to ask Happy for her opinion. Happy's extraordinary sixth sense was so special at routing out the cause of a suspicious circumstance.

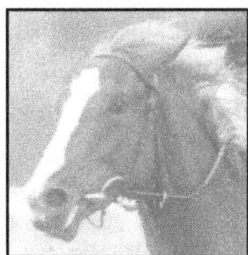

12

Whitey dead! His kind heart stopped like a dropped metronome. He'd moved quickly when I suggested we swap Derby hopefuls. He must have searched in the owners and trainers manual to find the list of Ivor's owners, and contacted several before he got a prompt response from my Canadian owner, who was willing to make a trade.

I worried for Lonelyheart, hoping that Whitey's head lad would be up to the job of training him to achieve his destiny.

When I returned from Lingfield I found Happy devastated. She wept for Whitey, she prayed for him. She mumbled, "Such a gorgeous man. So healthy looking, never complained, except about a headache."

Headache! A light went on in my brain. It was like in a cartoon when a light bulb, surrounded by sparks, is over someone's head.

I wanted to follow that light to a logical conclusion, but all at once my circumstances changed drastically. Hal Murphy, my Canadian owner who also owned the acreage of Ivor's yard and the gallops, arrived in London. He asked me to come to see him right away in his suite at the Claridge's Hotel. He had urgent business to discuss regarding Anchor.

No contest. This was one owner I really had to please. Make no mistake. His Anchor, the finest American-bred horse in my yard, was the subject of our urgent business. Oh, God! What now?

Train from Epsom to London, taxi to Claridge's, elevator to the Murphy suite and there he was, Hal Murphy, the owner. I'd brought a bottle of Glenfiddich for him because Ivor had once mentioned he was keen on malt whiskey. How I wished he'd down the bottle's entire contents and become too drunk for serious conversation. But he didn't even open the bottle.

He held an open can of Diet Coke in his left hand while he gave me a high five with his right. I'd heard he was a rough customer, but in what way? I would soon find out.

In an unnecessarily loud voice for his small suite, he shouted, "Rick, I'm taking Anchor away from you if he's not entered in a big stakes race. I want a diamond-encrusted trophy! I want to equal the Aga Khan's win last year with his Azamour. Not to mention the one million pounds in prize money. That would help to pay your bills too!"

His enormous laugh sounded like icebergs ripping off a glacier.

What could I say? I'd been the first person to suggest that Anchor might be a candidate to win a stakes race. And Anchor had won at Royal Ascot, which proved he liked the course. But Anchor had won a five-thirty, at the end of a long day. Never the time of day of the major races. Most importantly: Anchor's a sprinter.

I tried flattery. "You chose a fine yearling when you bought Anchor, Mr. Murphy. He --"

"You're telling *me*?" Another huge guffaw. I thought if he yelled any louder the neighbors in the next door suites would certainly complain to the front desk.

I tried history. "That race is traditionally won by classic-distance horses that became legends: Nijinsky, Shergar, Nashwan. I don't think -"

He interrupted again with more guffaws, and more icebergs cracking off a glacier. "Yeah, and Swain, Dancing Brave, Montjeu and Galileo. Don't imagine I haven't read the list of the greatest winners, too. And I want Anchor right up there with that lot. Are you gonna get him there? Or do I have to put some other trainer in charge of the yard?"

I breathed hard. I said nothing. I delved into my briefcase and drew out photographs of Anchor winning his Ascot five-thirty race. He'd won by a nose, with two contenders almost at the wire with him. I sighed meaningfully. Then I said, "It was a close thing, Mr. Murphy. With another jockey, he might have been beaten."

"And what jockey have you booked to ride him?" No guffaws this time. Murphy's expression had become deadly.

"No one yet, Sir. Most of the top contenders come from yards that have their own stable jockeys under contract. We don't have that luxury. And, with all due respect, I have reservations about Anchor taking a race that isn't a sprint, even if we could get someone as good as Kieren Fallon."

"You haven't heard a word I've said, Harrow. Anchor's running in the stake race I suggested. Have you entered him?"

"Well, yes. Sure. You asked me to a long time ago. So of course I did. But Mr. Murphy, I must tell you that Anchor's recent performance tells us he can win at major racecourses but in the smaller races. And if we burn him up by running him on July 29, he may never win anything again. He's your horse. I'll follow your orders. But in fairness to Anchor, I had to tell you the truth."

Now his suite *was* a glacier. A long silence. The bottle of Glenfiddich was opened, and two glasses were taken from the suite's bar. Mr. Murphy handed me a glass and said, "No ice, but then you Brits don't take ice with your drinks. I've always liked you, Rick. And I like you even more now that you've spoken the truth and not sucked up to me with promises of what can't be."

"Sorry, I couldn't have held out some hope. My suggestion is that we put him in on the July 28th Charity Day. There's a small race; that will suit him."

"You aren't running anything on July 29?"

"Again, I'm going to be totally frank with you. Yes, I'm running a horse in the International Handicap on the 29th - that mad cavalry charge - it will just suit another horse in our yard better. He loves the gallop up Ascot's straight."

Mr. Murphy slumped into the sofa. He grabbed a cushion and hugged it as if for security. "Yeah, that's horseracing! I spend the money and some other lucky guy's horse goes for a big one. I say, let's party! Let's cheer ourselves up with a whopper of a fiesta. Will you organize that? Maybe you do better at party planning than with horse training."

I gave a thin laugh, and escaped as quickly as was feasible from the suite.

How to arrange a party? On short notice? And who would be the guests? In mid-July, London empties out with its denizens rushing to St. Tropez, Antigua, or Bangkok. I'd lost contact with people I'd known at school, or in my regiment.

All the way back to Epsom, I listened to the train's wheels grinding "guests, guests, guests."

My solution was waiting for me at home: Ellie Grace. She was babysitting while Happy and Mrs. Roe had gone shopping for baby clothes and other necessities.

"Ellie! I need your help."

"Isn't it enough that I've changed Tim's diapers twice already?"

"I'm talking about a different kind of help. I've been ordered by my most important owner, the Canadian, to give a smash party. I think he wants it for Ascot's summer fixtures week. There's very little time to get a guest list together. And I can't think of a soul to invite."

"What fun! Here, you take Tim. It's all right, he's dry. And let me find a pencil and paper. Now, first of all, we need to have a royal. Maybe the Michaels of Kent. You know him from your regiment, don't you?

"Regiment? Yes, but we only met at a joint forces party."

"Good. The Kents, they'll come. And we need someone from the entertainment world. Elton John. Know him?"

"No."

"Pater knows him; they're on some charity board together. And a movie star: Madonna, Gwyneth Paltrow, or Kate Winslet? Mater adores films. I'm sure she knows one of them."

"And where are we giving this party? He's at Claridge's, so it might make sense to give it there. Even The Queen has given parties there."

"I think a social unknown needs to try something more unusual. New. Or else very distinguished," Ellie said.

"How about a tent near the boathouse of the Serpentine? Memories of King George IV, telling the talented child-artist, Millais, that he could swim there as often and for as long as he wished."

"No, been done too many times. Wait. I know! Spencer House. Centrally located,nicely refurbished by the Rothschilds who have it on a long lease. Expensive, but worth every farthing. Great hors d'oeuvres, and the best champagne. We'd have to use the house caterer because they don't want the standard to slide."

"I've been there, as a visitor. It's perfect!"

"Oh, it's not the same when you're there for a party! I went to Ted Turner's fete for the CNN London crew. It was on Guy Fawkes night, and there were wonderful fireworks along the terrace. Another time I went in full daylight, and the guests moved from one caviar station to another, set up along the terrace. It was divine. We'll get some lovely music, and a great P.R. person to write up the event. No scurrilous, unflattering press for this party."

Happy and Mrs. Roe entered through the doorway, their arms peppered with tiny packages for Tim. "What's this I hear, 'our party' and 'unflattering press'? Didn't you go see Hal Murphy? What'd he say about Anchor not running in a stakes race? Did we lose Murphy?"

"Murphy was far from delighted. But agreed to the smaller race on Friday. Right now, he just wants a party. Don't ask me why. He just wants to party. And Ellie has agreed to help me arrange it."

"Can I help in any way? Don't know that I could make up much of a guest list, but --"

"Happy, my love, your job is to get the best possible jockey for Anchor."

"Kieren Fallon! If he ain't - I mean isn't - already booked, or banned still from UK courses."

Tim interrupted our making any more plans. He started to howl for his supper like a puppy locked outside in the rain.

102

Later that night, in our double bed, I mulled over the day's events. Happy, so heavily pregnant, had lost much of her libido. Sex had become a rarity. She had pains in her legs, back and abdomen. I could only hope her libido would return after the new baby's birth, as it had after Tim's.

I wondered, had Murphy been testing me? Surely he'd been getting plenty of information about Anchor from our head lad, Tom. I knew they communicated by e-mail, FAX and cell phone. Ivor had hired Tom years ago about the same time as the yard was set up. Lucky I told Murphy the truth. Otherwise I might be out of a job.

The following afternoon I drove to London in our rental car. When I arrived at Claridge's, the doorman appeared promptly. His high hat held by his free hand against a sudden wind. I gave him the car, which he dispatched to the hotel garage by a uniformed minion. Entering Claridge's hall, I strode confidently up its short flight of steps but my well-being slumped like a sail in an unexpectedly calm sea when I caught a glimpse of Hassan lounging next to the piano where a trio played for guests having tea. Hassan saw me and quickly approached. How I would have liked to avoid him, but it wasn't possible.

"Hello, old chap." His voice sounded like waves crashing against a rocky shore: the fake Oxford accent very pronounced. Heads turned. People thought there was about to be an unpleasant confrontation. "I've just been upstairs with your friend Mr. Hal Murphy."

Not *owner* but *friend*.

"Uh, you have?"

"Charming fellow. First class, for a Canadian. We talked horses, of course."

"Of course."

"Actually, I'm here at Claridge's to see Sheik Abdullah bin Hamad Al Khalifa."

"The son of Bahrain's king, who's said to be the world's richest man. The Sheik could afford very costly horse flesh."

"Yes, indeed. But sadly, he isn't interested in becoming one of my owners. He's entirely besotted with music. Only lately, March in fact, his Bahrainian guest, Michael Jackson, announced he'll be recording another all-star charity single. The Sheik was given 'the pleasure' of announcing it to the Associated Press. The song's titled "I Have This Dream." Wonderful! So far, Jackson's booked Snoop Dogg, Ciara, Keyshia Cole, James Ingram, Jermaine Jackson, Shanice and the Reverend Shirley Caesar with the O'Jays. However, Michael Jackson still wanted to include more singers, so the release date isn't firm yet."

I hadn't a clue who these singers he mentioned were, other than the Jacksons. I smiled politely, but the smile was very weak. "I guess it's something along the lines of Bob Geldorf's record "Do They Know It's Christmas?"

"Exactly. Brilliant maneuver on Michael Jackson's part. Now that he's living in Bahrain, you know."

I didn't. My smile went even weaker this time.

Heading toward the lift, its doors flung open by a flunky in a Claridge's uniform, I tried casually to end this unwanted meeting. "See you, Hassan." But, just as the doors were about to close again with me inside, in pushed Sirena. I hadn't noticed, but she was lurking in the side hall. She smiled like a snake that had just swallowed a mouse. "Oh, what a surprise! Are you going up to see Hal Murphy, too?"

For one instant I wondered if she needed a male escort to use this elevator, in order not to be perceived as a hotel hooker. Would this chance meeting instead place me in the role of her pimp? I said, "Hello, Sirena. I didn't expect to see you here. In case you've forgotten, I'm very much in love with my wife. And, yes, I'm going up to see Mr. Murphy. I train his British runners, you know."

I said the last few words rather loudly for the benefit of the elevator operator. I hoped my clothes - more high stable than Bond Street - would offer proof of my status.

Sirena's individual perfume swirled from her clothes. She swung into an angelic pose and countered, "Yes, and I'm here to offer him a really great colt Hassan knows about. He wants two million pounds for it. But I'm sure he'd accept one million if you'd be the trainer. Then Murphy could be sure to win back his purchase price."

I swallowed hard, and that wasn't all that was hard about me, I did the gentlemanly thing and allowed Sirena to leave the elevator and walk ahead of me down the corridor.

Hal Murphy stood in the open doorway of his distinguished suite. Today he wore cotton trousers and a T-shirt, with loafers. His suite, beautifully decorated with authentic French antiques, had no air conditioning. He greeted us simultaneously. "Come in, Miss Sirena. And Rick! Sorry it's so hot in here, but I've opened all the windows. Come stand beside one."

He positioned himself against the wall beside the wider of the suite's windows. His back rested against the wall which provided a cool shield against the late-afternoon heat.

Sirena shook her head "no thanks" to the offer of a window. She draped her back against the velvet cushions of the larger of two sofas. Heat didn't bother *her*. Oh, no! She was the one who usually generated heat. "I've brought you the pictures of the colt you requested, Hal."

Hal, not Mr. Murphy.

"Yeah," he grunted. "Show them to Rick. He's my trainer. He'll have to decide if we should buy the colt. What's his price?"

"Two million."

"Pounds, or Canadian dollars?"

"Pounds."

"Too steep for me. Better tell Hassan to offer it to one of his Arab owners."

"He hasn't any. No Arabs. Not yet. He's working on that. Hassan's owners are mostly American or British." She was careful not to mention just how many Americans, or how may British owners he had.

I hoped that was the end of their dialogue, and that Sirena would get up from the sofa and leave. No tea or drinks had been offered to her.

She stayed glued to the sofa like oatmeal paste on wallpaper.

Now it was to be my turn to have Hal Murphy's comments slide over me like the beam of a lighthouse. "Rick, you phoned to say you've got all the data for my party."

"I have what you wanted, I hope. I'm not a party planner. For that your best bet would be The Queen's second cousin, Lady Elizabeth Anson. She's the best. But my neighbor, Ellie Grace, has come up with some good ideas, and a great guest list. Her parents' and her countess grandmother's friends. Ellie suggested Spencer House for the venue, which has great appetizers and champagne, and maybe fireworks. But it all depends if the place is already booked."

"I know about Spencer House. I walked through it as a tourist. A gorgeous job the Rothschilds did on restoring it back to peak condition. Try for it, whatever the cost."

"Ten thousand pounds for the use of the house, plus the appetizers and champagne."

"Okay. And if we can't get it, I've thought about contacting my Canadian High Commissioner. He has a beautiful building on Grosvenor Square. But, again, it would depend on the date and if the High Commissioner would be willing. I am a big tax-payer, you know."

"Ellie thought about borrowing an embassy. But with so many national holidays being in the month of July, embassies are usually giving parties of their own."

"Got it. Okay. What about the date?"

I hesitated to give him the suggested date, with Sirena listening to our every word. I worried she might give this information to Hassan and that the two of them would crash our party. I had no intention of exposing Hal Murphy to these two any more than was strictly necessary.

Hal put my worry to rest like a kindly father settling his child in a cradle. "We can discuss that later. After Miss Sirena leaves. Which I believe should be about now." In a courtly but determined manner he offered her his arm and led her back to the corridor.

Returning to his favored place, reclining again on a wall near the widest open window, Hal added, "Mrs. Murphy arrives tomorrow. And I sure don't want her to smell that woman's perfume permeating this place. She'll howl like a shot bear."

Confidently, I suggested Ellie's two possible dates. "The best would be at the very beginning of the summer Ascot meeting. The eve of it, in fact."

Hal Murphy agreed to the first proposal. I didn't need to get to the second. He showed me the door, too, but not by taking my arm. Instead he held out a hand for the envelope that contained all the data we'd collected to make sure his party went well. Then we each said a brief goodbye.

Down in the lobby, I hoped to avoid Sirena. No way. I had to wait for my car to be brought back from the hotel garage, so she had plenty of time to trap me.

"Oh Rick, seems there's not a taxi in sight. I imagine all the taxi drivers have gone to tea. Or else they're saving their gas for the theatre-goers. Will you drive me to The Dorchester? The hotel has plenty of parking spaces in front and you could come upstairs for a drink in my suite!"

What to say?

"Sorry, Sirena. I promised Happy I'd pick up some special baby things for Tim," I lied. "I may have to try all sorts of shops." I took a deep breath. "You've only a five minute walk to The Dorchester."

My car arrived and I left Sirena to slither away to The Dorchester, alone.

13

Hassan and Sirena crashed the Murphy's party anyway.

I figured out that my assistant trainer yearned for a roll-in-bed with Sirena, and she worked it so that he told her the date and the venue. Poor Burp hadn't a hope in hell that Sirena would ever give him a bonk, but, Crist-on-a-bike, he wouldn't give up trying.

Crist-on-a-bike! Oh, now I've caught that damned expression of Burp's. He wouldn't go to the Murphys' party because he didn't have the right clothes. But I suspect he felt he'd be out of his depth socially, rather like a dolphin among sharks.

Hassan had no such scruples. He arrived in his rented Daimler, with footman as well as a chauffeur. Sirena startled us all by coming dressed as a Turkish princess, in an authentic outfit fit for a harem: purple velvet, embroidered neck to hem with gold thread. Instead of a veil across her nose, she wore a Georgian tiara attached to heavy draperies that followed her footsteps in a regal train. As usual, she had doused herself with her signature Oriental perfume.

Happy gave her a disapproving look worthy of a no-hoper that failed at the most minor of racecourses. Now, enormous when seen from the front due to her advanced pregnancy, Happy managed to be photographed from the shoulders up for our publicity. Her picture duly appeared in the *Tatler*, *Harpers Queen*, *The Daily Mail* and *The Express*. *The Times* ran a photo of our royal guest. *The Spectator* featured our politician. *The Daily Telegraph* used an old portrait of our noble Duke. Madonna and Elton John were mentioned as no-shows in *Private Eye*.

Our P.R. guy did the Murphys proud. A good investment.

Hassan boomed out to his unwilling host, "Hal, you really must go see that colt I told you about. His price has been reduced to only a million and a half --"

"Reduced only because he's not worth the two million," Murphy snapped back curtly, his eyes as steely as an ironmonger's at a forge.

Trying to be clever, I interrupted, "That figure, two million, rings a bell. One of your Arab horsemen paid that amount for a racehorse that's now used to rake the grass after races."

Hassan shot down my remark like a Nazi Wehrmacht war plane machine gunning a British Hurricane. "Rick, you're a dear boy, but you really don't know much about buying horses. I recall you bought Nile to run in the classics, but he turned out to go no more than seven furlongs."

I swallowed hard. No reply to that.

Clara Murphy, a kindly woman, but somewhat crippled by rheumatoid arthritis, chimed in, "Our Rick didn't have a chance to retrain Nile. Hal and I both know that story. You might say, right from the horse's mouth." Looking at her curved spine and arms hampered by elbow crutches, I wondered how Hal had been able to turn seductive Sirena away. True love takes many forms.

110

The Murphys had opted to stand in the Library under an imposing line of ancient portraits. Their royal invited guest had kindly agreed to stand in the line with them to receive their guests. My contribution to the guest list had been all of my present owners. In addition were the Hugh Gordons, who had taken their horse away from me but were now negotiating to return him because he'd lost so much condition. Also, I invited the David Bonds, who had included us in a fantastic party they gave to celebrate their son, James's, twenty-first birthday. They'd leased a castle in Berwick and provided guns for everyone to shoot Scottish grouse on its moor, like their friend Antony Roberts.

Personally, I don't shoot birds. I don't shoot, period. When I was twelve, my father introduced me to the sport as a sort of fertility rite. He took me to the Scottish Highlands to stalk deer. But when I saw how much a yearling deer looks like a yearling horse, I couldn't shoot it. And have never shot anything since then.

Most of the guests swirled in groups near the two bars, but there was one unpleasant confrontation in the entrance hall. That took place when Sirena swept in, uninvited, in her over-the-top Turkish costume. Ascot race-goers are accustomed to seeing foreigners in their national garments - African women with color-streaked swaths of fabric on their heads; Mongolians in ankle-length embroidered coats matched with hats that featured eight-inch spikes; Pakistanis in silk trousers topped by knee-length jackets. But this was London, not Ascot. No, it was Sirena's outrageous flirting with her husband that sparked Mrs. Hugh Gordon's fury. The Gordons said they were returning their horse to my stable because it "lost condition." I was pretty certain the real reason was that Mrs. Gordon had caught Sirena at her ploys - and play.

Mrs. Gordon had called Sirena a tart! Sirena bleated back in Turkish. It was a distasteful harangue. Happy stepped in like a coach during a disputed play at a football game.

"How lovely that you've come to the party," Happy cooed to Mrs. Gordon in her best elocution style. "You're the best-dressed lady here! Please come upstairs with me, there's a room I want you to see. It's a tropical garden with palm trees. Only these trees are covered in gold leaf." She actually pulled Mrs. Gordon out of the hall and up the main circular staircase, leaving Sirena alone, bereft of any reason to misbehave further.

I can thank Happy for avoiding a worse scene, especially if Mrs. Gordon had continued with her accusations of Sirena in front of our all-important guest, the Royal.

Following the example of our Royal by eight o'clock, most of the guests had left. They had other parties to go to, London-style dinners for which they couldn't be late. But I still had vital work to do - talk to my principal owners about their horses.

To Hugh Gordon, I said, "Thank you very much for returning your horse to our yard. I hope to restore him to top condition in time for Goodwood races. Unfortunately, there's not enough time for Summer Ascot's second Friday day."

Colonel Flyte didn't wait for me to come over to him. He grabbed my arm half-way through the exit door. "I've paid the entry fee for Friday's big race. Will Broadback be running?"

"I hope so." Nothing more. No promise. Broadback would run only if there was a downpour that day, and mud. He was definitely a mudder.

William and Beatrice wanted to know if BillandBea would compete on Saturday. No way. That horse needed a lot more condition. I was gentle with them, "BillandBea needs a little more training." Carefully, I compared him to the Gordons' colt, which, they knew, was the finest English-bred horse in my yard. "He'll be best at Goodwood," I assured them.

When all the guests had left, I took the host aside. "Anchor should win his race on Friday. But I've entered Broadback in the same race. He's a mudder. Please don't be angry."

My genial owner laughed kindly; he was in a great mood after his successful party. "Why angry? You can't arrange the weather. I learned that long ago when I first raced in England. There's nothing you can do about the weather. But, Rick, I've always believed a really great horse can produce no matter what the weather."

"True. And on Friday we'll find out if Anchor really *is* a great horse."

On Friday, at early morning gallops, I scanned the sky and decided the weather could go either way. Come sun or rain, my two runners would be transported in the horsebox to Ascot.

Happy stopped me as we were about to leave. "I don't feel so good, Rick. I think I should stay close to home." She was wearing the same outfit she'd worn for Royal Ascot a month earlier. Only now it was beyond too tight. I was amazed she'd been able to zip up the zipper.

"My darling, my precious! I won't go either. I'll send Burp to delegate. He can belt up the horses, and take the prize if we win. I'm certainly not going to leave you alone when you don't feel well."

"I'm not alone. Mrs. Roe promised she'd stay with me, even though it is her day off."

"I can't leave you. I won't leave you."

"But you must leave, and right away."

She pushed me into the driveway, and threw my old brown porkpie into the car. No tall hat or tailcoat today, just a normal suit and the typical trainer's hat.

No contest. I'd learned early on in our marriage back at her Paw's Kentucky homestead: there was no arguing with Happy.

I'd forgotten what a carnival atmosphere Ascot has on Charity Day. County matrons fielded stalls selling charity buttons and cards. There were games to play for a good bit of money. Debutantes wandered through the crowds with baskets to collect money for the charities.

But for my owners the atmosphere was grim. The weather kept skipping from sunlight to clouds like a day on the Irish moors. Anchor looked magnificent in the paddock, his pelt shining, his ears pricked, and his legs waiting for action.

I'd scratched Broadback because even if rain pelted down, there was no guarantee the stretch would be muddied in time.

Captain Flyte looked furious. Would I lose him as an owner? I knew he was a cheapo, and it would be bitter about paying the entry fee only to have his horse scratched on the day of the race. And Hal Murphy; would he still be a genial owner if Anchor failed dismally?

Anchor didn't fail. He won.

Hal and Clara Murphy glowed like fireflies on a summer's night. There was no trophy presentation but they did receive what they craved - a wave of turf reporters inquiring about Anchor's future plans. Hal turned to me, "Ask my trainer," he said with a grin.

I handled those toughies as carefully as I would newborn chicks. "Maybe a race on St. Leger Day," I tentatively said.

114

From close by I felt a douse of hatred. I turned: Colonel Flyte, leaning over the rails, had heard my statement about the St. Leger.

Loud enough for the jackal reporters to hear, he blurted, "You promised that Broadback would run at Doncaster."

With a forced grin, I carefully said, "And so he might. Not in the St. Leger, but in a good race at Doncaster.

Thankfully, Hal and Clara Murphy grabbed my arm and sailed me through the crowds of well-wishers,and took me to the nearest champagne bar, leaving the blustering Colonel in our wake.

Had I escaped Colonel Flyte's wrath, or merely postponed it? I wasn't to know that for several weeks to come. But within the hour I had a far more pressing reason for anxiety.

Happy, unable to reach me, made a cell phone call to Ellie's cousin, Viscount Jeremy Grace, who was also at Ascot. I was downing my second Buck's Fizz - orange juice and other goodies in champagne - when he grabbed my arm,and pulled me aside rather roughly.

Outfitted like the country gentleman he was, Jeremy Grace was wearing corduroy slacks and a blazer, hardly suitable for Ascot on Charity Day. In a desperate tone he said, "Happy called me to find you. She might be having labor pains. You'd best be getting back to Epsom."

Concerned, the Murphys accepted the reason for my sudden departure. But Hassan didn't, and waylaid me at the owners and trainers car park. "I hear you're worried that Happy may be going into labor. Take it from a pro, it's far too soon for that. I know just the thing. Give her some aspirin." He handed me a small bottle. I popped it into my jacket pocket, and without a backward glance found my car.

As I sped down the driveway, I felt like Lancelot going to rescue Guinevere. But she wasn't in our cottage, so I headed for the stables where I found Happy overseeing the evening meals. Gone were her pains; her face was radiant. "I heard Anchor won. I knew he would. He told me so this morning. The Murphys must have been pleased. And I heard on the TV you're planning to send him to Doncaster. That's a big race. Maybe too big."

I grabbed Happy with both arms and pressed her to me, but not too hard. "You all right my precious girl?"

"Not so good couple hours ago. But now, I'm fine. I'm hungry. Come, let's go eat. What I wouldn't give for some grits and hushpuppies."

We ate watching the replay of Anchor's race on the nine o'clock news. My hint that Anchor might run in on St. Leger Day had been big news all over England.

I didn't like what I saw. Anchor was favoring his rear right leg. I hadn't noticed that when he was thundering towards the finish line, but it was obvious during the replay. "I'll defer to your advice on Anchor," I said, kissing Happy across the coffee table. "But for the time being I think we'd better concentrate on our runners for the Goodwood race."

Glorious Goodwood is a relaxed sort of meeting in Sussex. Held on the grounds of the Duke of Richmond's private estate, racegoers dress very casually, some even looking as though they're heading for a day at the beach. Ladies wear floppy straw hats of the garden variety and rope soled shoes. I hadn't expected that happy would make the long drive down to Hampshire for the first day of the meeting, but she surprised me, and had packed a picnic lunch for the three of us, Burp included. We didn't have a runner, so we joined the rollicking crowds huddled on a hillside for a free view of the course; there we ate our vittles.

It wasn't all picnic fun for me; I studied the condition of the course. Our runner was a sprinter and entered into the Stewards' Cup - a race with a long history of upsets. When there were many runners, they went down the course like a cavalry charge. I was hoping for a small field of horses so that our runner wouldn't be injured by being kicked, or receiving the whipping meant for another contender. Happy studied the course too. "I have a feeling, Rick, maybe it's not the right course for our runner."

I deferred to Happy's judgment and scratched Hugh Gordon's colt. But I left in BillandBea in a minor race because I felt if he didn't win a race pretty soon, he'd be sold out of our yard.

On the day of BillandBea's race there was a picnic atmosphere everywhere on the racecourse. The Duke of Richmond, with family members chortling and waving to friends from their private box, set the tone. There was a lot of laughter from the bars, and even the green pre-parade ground seemed less anxious than usual.

BillandBea didn't disgrace our yard. He looked healthy, alert and ready to take on whatever came. His owners, glowing with anticipation - often the best part of racing - were both on hand to cheer him home. And cheer they did as he came in first. Goodwood *was* glorious for them. They were contented owners.

I knew I wouldn't be losing Bill and Beatrice from my yard.

The only sour note on that day was the appearance of sultry Sirena in the bar, right when Bill and Beatrice were offering champagne to everyone.

Sirena, not to anyone's surprise, was incorrectly dressed for Goodwood. She wore the Royal Ascot-type hat with an exaggerated brim, and an organza dress fit for a cocktail soirée. She sidled up to me, took my glass of champagne and swallowed the contents, making sure I noticed she placed her lips on the glass where mine had left a mark.

Then, she took my free hand in hers and whispered, "I'm still at The Dorchester."

No whisper from me. I boomed, "Happy, time for us to leave. We can't stay away from Tim any longer." I took Happy's arm and marched out of the bar, leaving Bill and Beatrice rather startled.

Meanwhile, Doncaster and its great St. Leger - a classic race dating from the early eighteenth century - loomed closest. From 1778 it had been prominent on the racing calendar, run on the new Town Moor course for three-year-olds over two miles. In 1813 the race was reduced to one mile six furlongs and a hundred and ninety-three yards.

I had serious work ahead of me. I needed to prepare Broadback, and most especially our main hope Anchor, right away.

And I hadn't overlooked a chance at Doncaster for Feathers, either.

He would be heading north with his pet cat Bumbles, too.

Doncaster itself, dating back before 1600, had seen all kinds of peculiarities in horses, but one with a pet cat was probably a first!

I thought that Doncaster's broad galloping track would suit Feathers. Unlike Epsom - with its ups and downs and sharp corners - Doncaster was more like a Newmarket racecourse and it's hard to get better than that. Yes, Feathers had performed well at Lingfield course, which is an excellent trial for Epsom's harsh demands, but I'd grown very fond of my American import and wanted Feathers to have an easier race than the track at Epsom would afford.

So it was that Happy and I drove to the north lands where race-goers truly love the sport. There, ladies come out to the course to cheer home the winners, not to show off their hats. Their husbands and lovers are as tough as Epsom's corners, yet warmhearted where horses are concerned. But these heavy drinking and big betting northerners were not about to overlook any failing in my string.

Disaster hit me from a different direction in the owners and trainers car park. Colonel Flyte scolded me loudly in front of the north's major players. "You let me down. I told you I wanted Broadback to run in the St. Leger. But no, you put him in a two-bit race. And what have we had? Non-stop rain all week so the course is awash with the mud he loves! Damn fool, you."

Flyte always treated me like a groom, but not in front of people who mattered to me. Not good! Among the crowd were at least two owners who had considered coming to my yard.

What could go wrong, went wrong. I don't mean to grumble, because we didn't have vital calamities such as a horse breaking a leg, or our jockey smashing a collarbone. The majority of my miseries, as Happy put it, were simply caused by embarrassment.

I invited Happy and Burp for lunch in the main dining room. A gloomy place which couldn't compare with Ascot and Goodwood's new facilities. Neither of my owners there that day were generous enough to provide lunch for us. Colonel Flyte seemed to consider me his social inferior and wouldn't be seen eating at the same table, unless I was footing the bill in a place such as the Turf Club.

The Murphys were entertaining close friends from Canada, very rough types, whom they may have thought 'not quite my cup of tea.'

When the bill arrived for our meals, neither Burp nor I had enough money to pay it. Happy had to count out spare coins from the bottom of her handbag to ante up the amount. In the pre-parade ring Happy slipped in the mud and her heavily pregnant form slid a yard before we could help her to her feet. Her maternity dress was ruined. Where was she going to find another at the Doncaster track? There was no other option for her but to return to our car and crouch there for the remainder of the afternoon wearing only her clean maternity slip and my old blazer.

Anchor won his race. Broadback didn't. Another embarrassment of a different sort. Because the Murphys now considered they did indeed have a 'great' horse, one which should have been entered in the Steward's Cup at Goodwood.

Colonel Flyte vented all the piss from his pot of fury on me. Like a spoiled brat in a posh nursery, he shouted, "I always took you for a damn fool. Out of commiseration over Ivor's suicide, I stayed in your stable. But you can be jolly sure I'm leaving it now. I'll send for my horse in the morning." His tirade was delivered pointedly in front of his Jockey Club friends, for the piss to sting more.

There was one saving moment. Captain Ainsley joined us in that muddy car park and tapped on the window of our car. "Rick, old boy. I've given some thought to Feathers, and I've decided to buy him from Hal Murphy. After all, he was just a trade Whitey arranged in exchange for Lonelyheart. Hal Murphy was just being kind. He will, of course, remain in your yard." Feathers had been scratched from his race, and was on his way home with Bumbles. The going had been too heavy for him and I didn't want to risk his future rating.

We shook hands on the deal. He strode away, smiling pleasantly.

"That's one fine gentleman," Happy sung out. The painful incident with Colonel Flyte, although certainly not forgotten, was somehow ameliorated. I'd been fired by one owner and had another owner extend his interests.

I'd seen the mean side of Colonel Flyte before, when he's snubbed Captain Ainsley for having come up through the ranks. But, today, when he berated me in front of his Jockey Club friends, could there have been a darker suggestion in that spate of words? Could he had been insinuating that I'd been bought by gangsters to make Broadback run below form in some sort of crooked betting coup?

My anxiety was such that I failed to notice how Happy had begun to shiver. Her maternity slip was not much protection from the night air. My old blazer was the only comfort she had.

"I need something to drink. Could we stop along the road?" she asked, between hiccups that suddenly had grabbed her swollen body. "And "I found a bottle of aspirin in your coat pocket. I'd take one if I had some water."

We stopped at a service station. Happy disappeared into the ladies' room and I went to the counter for Coca Colas for the three of us to drink in the car.

Arriving home there was more unpleasantness. Tim had been bawling for hours, and Mrs. Roe threatened to quit. I cradled our infant in my arms and he stopped wailing temporarily. As soon as I tried to leave him alone, he started bawling again. I told Mrs. Roe to go to bed and brought a cot into Tim's room to sleep beside him. No complaint from Happy. She was too tired and wet and miserable after six hours of driving and four hours of being soaked in mud.

The next morning it wasn't our colts that had sprung fevers. It was Happy.

"I meant to take an aspirin but I left that bottle from your coat pocket in the bathroom at the service station and we don't have any left. Please, darlin', will you go to town and get me some?"

I did. I cleaned the passenger seat of mud, and sped to a chemist's for aspirin and cough syrup and whatever else our pharmacist would approve for a very pregnant woman. Nothing worked. Happy lay alone in our bedroom for ten nights. Until time took its course and she bloomed again.

Ten nights without sex. To not dwell on that, I worked straight through. Burp and I drove to Newbury and watched BillandBea come in second in a minor race. I listened to his 'Crist-on-a-bike' until I thought I'd shake him.

We won a good race at Lingfield on its all-weather track, but most of my concentration centered on preparing Anchor for the big purse in Dubai.

Happy felt well enough that I couldn't refuse to let her accompany me to Dubai. I wondered if the airplane would permit such a heavily pregnant woman on board, but the United Emirates Airline was accustomed to women being enveloped in huge all-covering garments and didn't bat an eye at Happy's flowing maternity smock.

She made it to Dubai, after arranging for Ellie to supervise Mrs. Roe. I delegated Burp to work the horses left behind in the yard. But what was heart-wrenching was saying "goodbye for now' to Tim.

The Murphys didn't accompany their horse to Dubai. They returned to Canada, satisfied with the party they'd given in London and the one prize they'd won at summer Ascot.

14

Arriving in Dubai made me think I'd been transported to Mars in the year 2500. I certainly didn't feel like it was today on planet Earth. To being with, I'd never seen such a mix of nationalities. Dubai had very little trained manpower among its native-born population and had to import people who could do all the jobs from manual work to complicated high tech.

The few Dubai Emiratis I counted were either camel-drivers wearing jeans and T-shirts, or wealthy Arabs in white flowing cloaks and head-dresses secured with black circular headbands. Some of the rich Arabs drove around on electric golf carts despite this being an oil-rich nation.

Architecture was art gone crazy - as far away from Georgian as possible. There were buildings that went diagonally from base to forty or more floors until reaching a point in the sky. Our hotel was like a huge white bat with its wings circling in towards its minimalist entrance. It was short of rooms. Although I was paying for this out of my own pocket, we had to agree to take a suite. "I'll sleep on the couch in the living room," I said gently, not trying to reprove Happy for being so huge, but knowing that a queen-size bed would scarcely hold her big belly in comfort.

She agreed. We unpacked. Happy took advantage that the racing hadn't begun, and went to sleep.

I was on my way to the visiting racehorses facilities to check on Anchor, but I didn't make it past the hotel lobby.

"Hello! Rick, darling!" That familiar sultry voice stopped me as if I'd been Devon Loch in the Grand National. Sirena sidled next to me. "How lovely that we're staying in the same hotel."

Not a word from me. I tried to sidestep her and make a dash for the exit door.

But Hassan appeared, blocking my getaway. "Rick, old chap. Good to see you here. I've a photo upstairs of that colt I offered to Hal Murphy. The price is now down to one million. Dear Hal okayed the sale but only if you agreed. Come upstairs? Hal really insists you judge this horse."

Could I afford to fall from Hal Murphy's good graces? No!

I followed Hassan and Sirena upstairs to a double suite. He disappeared promptly after showing me a faded photograph of a mediocre horse. Sirena called to me from one of the bedrooms.

"Rick! I've tripped . . . and fallen on the floor! Help me up!"

I entered the bedroom. Sirena was, in fact, crumpled on the floor, on the other side of the bed. I had to follow her blast of exotic perfume to find her.

Sirena was lying on the floor totally naked and with legs open. She was no longer enticing me, she was inviting me. Sex! Right there and then! Horrified by her withered body, and pox that looked like leprosy, I rotated my stance like the hands of a clock gone mad, and bolted for the corridor faster than if I'd been racing in the derby.

126

I hurtled back to our suite to tell Happy how much I loved her. Happy was gone. On her pillow was a note scrawled in red ink: Your wife will not be yours again until you buy the horse!

Under the words was the Arabic lettering that meant nothing to me. I knew the note hadn't been penned by Hassan. He was Oxford educated and wrote with the same precise English that he spoke.

I picked up the telephone and dialed the front desk. I asked if the hotel detective had seen my wife leave. "No. No one had witnessed the removal of a white, very pregnant lady." I asked to be connected to the police. There was a wait until a translator could be located.

"My wife has been kidnapped," I said slowly, speaking very distinctly, making sure I'd be understood. "Please get someone on the case quickly."

"Your name?"

"Rick Harrow. Listen, my wife is missing. She's very-"

"Your wife's name?"

"Hillary. But she goes by 'Happy.' She's very pregnant."

"Nationality?"

"I'm British. She's an American."

"Please to inform respective Embassies." The phone went dead.

Try again? What for!

I did inform both Embassies. Again I was connected, both times, to some uncaring individual who took our names, the address of the hotel, and offered nothing further. What were they afraid of? That this would start a war with Dubai? It hadn't happened over the proposed sale of US ports to the UAE.

In desperation, I dialed the number of Hassan's suite through the hotel's intercom system.

127

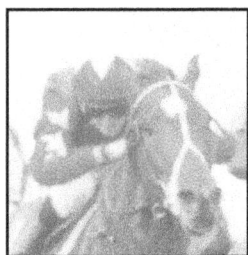

15

No answer in Hassan's suite. Not for a few minutes. But, finally, a heavily accented middle-European voice came on, "What you want? There's been a murder here and a gravely injured person. Get off the line. We need to speak to the police."

I recognized that voice. It belonged to the hotel's manager, Helmut Bokavitch. I'd met him at check-in and found him efficient, but not likeable. I breathed deeply, and asked, "Who's dead? Who's injured?"

Thinking, 'I pray God it isn't Hassan who's dead, because then how will I ever get a trace on my Happy?'

Bokavitch barked, "You know! You are on our sixth floor surveillance cameras. You were the last person to come out of the Hassan Mahmoud suite..."

Oh, God! Now I'm a murder suspect? *How can I hope to find Happy if they arrest me?* I whispered into the phone, "Please, tell me who has been killed! I promise you, I don't know anything."

"You promise? You! Open your door, I can see on my intercom that the police are there trying to enter."

They were there. Two tiny ape-like men in uniform, who had huge chests and very long arms. When I opened the door both men pointed guns at me. Within an instant I was handcuffed. They were stained with other people's blood. At first, I thought they were rusted, but a good look told me the color was dried blood!

Neither of the apes spoke English. They didn't need to; I was dragged along by the painful handcuffs. With my legs used to exercising horses, I managed to keep up as we entered the nearest elevator and went up to Hassan's floor.

A crowd of curiosity seekers had already accumulated in the corridor outside his suite. The police pushed them aside, but didn't enter the suite. Its door was strung with the yellow tape that internationally proclaims a crime scene.

Mr. Bokavitch looked down his fleshy nose at me, "You've been brought back to the scene of y our crime."

The curiosity seekers reveled in that information. But one of them spoke up in English, "Aren't you Rick Harrow, the trainer? Didn't I hear the dead woman invite you upstairs here to see a picture of a racehorse?"

I didn't reply. My heart was racing as soon as he'd said "dead woman."

Sirena! It meant that it was Sirena who was dead. Hassan was the 'injured' one. There was still a chance to get out of Hassan the location and identification of Happy's abductors. I turned to the one who'd addressed me in English, "Can you find out which hospital Hassan is in?"

"Give it a few minutes. The ambulance was slow to arrive, and he's only just been taken away. But, I think the ambulance came from a hospital named after the last Emir..."

"Don't tell him the name of the hospital," Bokavitch boomed. "He could go there and finish the job of killing him."

Bokavitch's attention was drawn away from me and my new friend who spoke English. He signaled to me with a wink while Bokavitch got down to serious talk with a fellow Serbian. The Serbian was another of the imports into Dubai's labor force; this one with the forensics lab. I caught a few words I recognized in the jabbering stream of Serbian: "Milosevic," and "massacres." The two Serbs were too caught up in the tales of their own country's murders to be bothered by this one.

I listened while they questioned a guest of the hotel. "Two shots. Loud as anything, like I wasn't in the next suite but in the next room. Ugly scream when the woman was hit. Apparently she dashed in front of this Hassan Mahmoud person, to shield him, and took the first shot. Killed her."

"Who was she?" asked another guest.

"A whore. One of those call-girls who hang around the lobbies of posh hotels." This, from a burly Irishman who no doubt had made use of any number of those call-girls.

Poor Sirena, I thought. At her finest hour she'd been relegated to a common whore at the very moment when she acted out the part of a heroine saving the life of her employer. Or pimp! To be more specific.

I didn't have much time to dwell on thoughts of Sirena. But still, as I was dragged along into the re-opened suite, past the yellow tape and plunged next to vast pools of blood, I did manage to recall that night in my home when she'd cooked in our kitchen with a dishcloth tied around her $1000 dress.

Bokavitch pointed to the nearest mess of blood. I thought that like Lady Macbeth, I could comment, "Yet who would have thought the old man to have had so much blood in him?" I could guess from Bokavitch's expression that he was mentally calculating how much a replacement rug would cost. "How did you clean off the blood that spattered on you? Better not have thrown your bloodied clothes down my hotel's laundry chute because we'll find them.

Having finally been invited to speak, I gave with a spate of words, "I left this suite before there was any blood. Look again at your security cameras, you'll see I left here in clean clothes. Then ask your telephone operator if I didn't put in three calls. One to the police to report that my wife had been kidnapped and to request help, and one to each of our respective embassies."

"We know about the telephone calls. Probably put in by an accomplice while you went back to the Hassan Mahmoud suite to do your dirty work."

Bokavitch's Serbian co-national had donned rubber gloves and was taking samples from the two pools of blood - one much smaller than the other.

Orders in Arabic to my two apes resulted in my being towed away from the crime scene. Out in the corridor my new friend called bout, "Emir Mohammed Hospital."

There wasn't anything I could do about going to that hospital, or anywhere else. The apes took me in a clamoring police car to a grim prison. I was booked. My watch, passport, money and shoes were taken from me. What I was to miss the most were the shoes.

I was placed in a smallish cell crowded with about thirty other suspected murderers, all of us standing because there wasn't room to sit or lie down. Some had urinated and emptied their bowels on the floor. We had to dirty our feet with their effluence.

I was in a cell for non-Muslims. The Muslims had larger cells so that they could face Mecca, kneel and pray five times a day. We saw bowls of water being carried to the Muslims, in order that they could wash five times a day before their prayers. If they had no other advantages, count the fact that their feet would remain clean.

Food came once a day: rice. The water was undrinkable: I used it to wipe my feet. We were permitted to go to the lavatory twice, once at dawn and once at sunset when all thirty of us lined up and waited our turn in front of the foul-smelling cubicle.

Fights broke out, but they didn't escalate because there was no space. One murderer would spit, or worse, at his neighbor, and there was name-calling which thankfully I couldn't understand. Sometimes a guard would come to the door of our cell and shout down the instigators. It was during one of the nastiest of those bouts that suddenly a ray of hope entered my life. I heard a British voice. The door swung open like that of a bank vault, and I was yanked outside into a corridor.

"BBC," the voice had announced. Once outside, he pulled me to one side and, while offering me a can of Coca Cola, said: "There's considerable interest in your case. We've been covering it for two days. I've brought my cameraman. Mind if we take a few?" He didn't elaborate further.

I hadn't shaved, or bathed, or brushed my teeth in the past two days. I felt ashamed contrasting my appearance, and probably my odor, to the neatly turned-out BBC man. He held out a beefy hand, "I'm Paul Moore. I realize you aren't looking your best, but that's good. It will elicit more sympathy."

"Please, tell me is there any news of my wife? Happy Harrow?"

"Nothing. she's disappeared off the face of this God-forsaken part of the Earth. But we did find out how she was taken out of the hotel."

"For God's sake! How?"

"I'm friends with a former M16 guy, Forbes Paltry. I often conscript him. He doesn't need the money because he works as one of the local potentate's bodyguards. He helps me out from time to time."

"So, how was it done? What did this M16 guy find out? Happy would never have just..."

"She was rolled up in a rug. Cleopatra style. Seems that many tourists buy handmade rugs when they visit this country. It's big business here. And they have their rugs delivered to their hotels. Your hotel's parcels man let two guys go upstairs to deliver a rug. It went to your suite. I checked that out on the tape in the surveillance camera on your floor."

"This Forbes Paltry, did he get any leads to where my Happy could be?"

"Not yet. And Forbes knows the back alleys and souks very well indeed. But no gossip about a pregnant white woman in any of them. Nothing at all."

"Oh,God. What can I do, stuck here in prison? And not a single lead?"

"Your story has been broadcast internationally for two days. Our office has been inundated with e-mails. One I've seen personally came from a Canadian, from that multi-millionaire, Hal Murphy. He instructed us to go see you in prison and tell you to pay the abductors the $1 million demanded for the horse."

"Dear, wonderful Hal! Would that I could accept his offer. But I can't. My conscience and my ethics just won't permit me to do that. And how I would love to! That nag isn't worth more than three or four hundred pounds at the most. The horse in the picture the abductors left behind isn't the first horse Sirena offered Hal in London, which was a racehorse with decent blood lines. The horses have been switched.

"Mr. Harrow, take the million! Pay the bastards. Get your wife released before..." He didn't spell out what we both knew could happen. "Listen to people who have experience in this sort of thing."

The corridor became more crowded.

"Is that Rick Harrow?" It was tall, elegantly dressed, Paul Moore, the British Vice-Consul. Then another voice, with a mid-Western American twang, said, "I'm Virgo Mora, with CNN. What's this vulture been telling you?" The new arrival was a fat short man. He glared at Paul Moore, and tried to push him aside to establish a position for his cameraman. The CNN camera was already rolling before I answered.

"Yes, I'm Rick. What's left of him. But there's nothing new for CNN to broadcast. I'll be going back to my cell within minutes, without any relief or hope."

The American snorted. "Back to your cell? Hasn't the great and noble Paul Moore told you? You've been sprung. Look! He's coming with your release papers. And the guard, that horror, has your wallet, your watch and your passport."

Virgo Mora was right. Elegant, distinguished looking Paul Moore, who could have passed for a Cabinet Minister, had led me on to embellish his story and had concealed the news of my release.

Relieved as I was, I still scrutinized the face of this Vice-Consul, waiting for him to say a few words in order to identify himself as the nerd who had been so short with me when I telephoned the embassy to report Happy's kidnapping.

When he finally spoke I learned he was not the same man; he had a broad Yorkshire accent and was not arrogant. On the contrary, he had an endearing humility. Better, he'd arrived carrying a pair of new leather slippers - of the type sold in the souks - and offered them to me so that I wouldn't ruin my own shoes with the urine and excrement on my unwashed feet. No doubt he'd brought slippers to other accused murderers and knew their need for saving their shoes. The Vice-Consul had no news of Happy for me, but Virgo Mora had plenty. He was willing to tell me all he knew in exchange for a ride back to my hotel in the consulate's car.

The strangest news came out first. Virgo smirked, grinning broadly, "You were filmed on Hassan Massoud's private camera, set up in that Sirena gal's bedroom. Not the same as the hotel's security video. You can be seen entering the bedroom, fully clothed, you sidestep a pile of her clothes, the camera shifts its focus to Sirena lying on the floor with her legs open. And then you scuttle away like a cockroach running from a broom.The video's timed. The entire scene takes less than a minute. So you're off the murder charge. But, if this hadn't been recorded, your fellow trainer Hassan could have taken you for a tidy sum. Blackmail."

"Hassan knows I don't have any money to spare. We're living on the edge."

"But your multi-millionaire owners have plenty. And what about the rumor that Hal Murphy has offered to give you the $1 million to buy that questionable horse?" He spoke as if to him $1 million was a very large sum.

I thought long before replying because I knew Virgo was primarily a journalist, and that anything I said to him would be broadcast on CNN.

His next slice of news was as comforting as my first cup of coffee, offered to me silently by the Vice-Consul,who was ready with a thermos full.

Virgo said, "Two of your pals from the UK arrived at your hotel this morning,The Hon. Eleanor Grace, and her Viscount cousin Jeremy." Virgo rolled the titles on his tongue like chocolate candy.

Ellie! With news of Tim? And who was overseeing Mrs. Roe if Ellie was here? And why Jeremy? Nice guy, but of what use under the present circumstances?

I learned the answers to those questions the instant I entered the hotel lobby. A group of newsmen and photographers huddled there, waiting for me, but I bypassed them, without a word or a smile, to greet the Graces.

"Ellie, so good of you to come. But who's staying with Tim?"

Huge hug from Ellie. "Tim's fine. Mrs. Ainsley called to say she'd watched the whole drama on the BBC and offered her services to stay with Mrs. Roe and Tim so that I could help you out here in Dubai.

"Jeremy, I don't know how to thank you for accompanying Ellie." We patted each other's shoulders.

In the hotel elevator, hoping to avoid security cameras, I asked Ellie, "Any more news from the kidnappers?"

"None. Not a word. It's worrisome. I don't want to alarm you further, but can it mean they no longer have Happy? Could she have been sold on to another gang?"

Quietly, Jeremy said, "I've spent years in Arab countries. Speak the language, know the customs. My intuition tells me that could be the case."

I turned to Virgo, "Don't broadcast that."

Virgo said, "No way. My cameraman left us after you got out of prison. I'm with you now as a friend."

Really? When Happy's abduction is a major story?

Vice-Consul Moore left me at the door of my suite. His parting favor was to give me a flask of scotch, a rarity in this Muslim country. "Remember you're British, keep a stiff upper lip," was his humble, low-key goodbye.

The return to my suite held mixed blessings. I felt like a schoolboy coming home from a bad trip. I missed Happy's ever-cheerful presence.

I welcomed the possibility of a bath. But there was urgent business to attend to.

"Jeremy, have you any idea how we can trace Happy's odyssey?"

Ellie went to the suite's no-alcohol bar and took out three mini bottles of orange juice. She poured the contents into glasses, one for each of us.

I hadn't given a thought to their thirst after the hot drive from the airport, or mine, after my release from the filthy prison.

Jeremy said, between rapid gulps of juice, "You know there are always loonies who come forward during situations like this. You may have read about some of them when the journalist Richard Perle was kidnapped." He failed to add, and was killed, his head lopped off in full view of a video camera, and the act broadcast worldwide. "I've contacted the BBC and CNN foreign office about ransom demands for Happy. None. But there were some of those usual loonies' ideas. One of which I believe could be promising. One suggested that you advertise in a local newspaper offering to meet the abductors' demand and buy the horse for $1 million."

"I can't do that. I haven't got $1 million, and I'm not going to accept Hal's offer and land him with a hopeless horse. Not right. And if I give counterfeit bills, or bars of gold-plated lead, what then. It could be the end of Happy when the kidnappers find the deal's a phony."

"The hell with what's right!" Ellie shouted across the room, as if I were on the other side of a stadium. "We're talking here about wonderful, loving Happy!"

138

"Don't think I don't anguish over that! In prison all that kept me standing,and not joining the corpses, was trying to workout how to save Happy. But I know we're up against some very able people. And I haven't figured out the way to deal with them."

Gently, Jeremy countered, "You don't deal with them.What good was dealing for Perle's family? Or so many others who've been murdered after kidnappings? Let me see the original note that the kidnappers left for you. Like millions of other people around the globe, I saw it reproduced on CNN. And I read Arabic script."

I murmured, "I never got that translated."

"Very simple. It said the same as the pigeon-English writing. Which, by the way, may have been faked. It seemed too obvious."

"Rick, I've worked in Arab countries for some years. And I've often heard Englishmen use pigeon-English as a ploy. Your abductors may be working for an Englishman."

"Or an Arab who knows English very well. It's got to be Hassan."

"Why? You've said yourself the horses have been switched. He may have been offering a perfectly genuine racehorse to Hal Murphy, admittedly, for an inflated price. But one with decent bloodlines, and acceptable conformation."

"The horse in that faded picture Sirena showed to me was that of a horse with donkey blood. But that's history. Now we haven't anyone to deal with, and no horse to trade $1 million for." I signed, then tried a grin. "Let me have a bath. I know I stink. No wonder Ellie's across the room."

Ellie smiled again in return. Her smile came out like tepid water on a sweltering hot day. She said nothing, instead walked into the bathroom and started the bath.

Jeremy looked dashed, as if he'd come to the edge of a cliff. "I'm sorry, devastated in fact, that I can't be of more help."

I said, "I think I should reconnect with the Vice-Consul, Paul Moore. He appeared amiable enough, and might go out of his way to help."

Ellie appeared at the bathroom doorway. She disagreed. "Don't want someone who helps with slippers and coffee. Forget going to a corporal when there's a general available. You must go straight to our ambassador to the UAE. Now he'd be someone worth approaching. My mater said she knows him."

Virgo, who'd kept silent while making notes, echoed: "UK's Ambassador. Great idea."

I left the three of them to thrash out that one, and rushed to the bathroom after collecting clean clothes. Bathed, shaved, and freshly dressed, I emerged into the sitting room to discover that my three visitors had disappeared. They weren't in the bedroom, the bed still unmade with Happy's body form marking the open sheets.

In another minute I heard their voices coming from a room adjacent to my empty sitting room. A door had been left ajar. I followed the voices. My three visitors were inspecting the room.

Jeremy explained, "According to CNN, all of this hotel's suites have three bedrooms, one on either side of the sitting room. Most of the hotel's guests are Arabs, and they often bring an extra wife or two with them, hence the second bedroom."

Virgo added, "One of the e-mails sent to CNN suggested that the killer could have entered Hassan's living room from an adjoining bedroom. That's why he didn't appear on the security camera that day. Having checked on the suite's location after

Hassan booked it, he could have been holed up in that room prior to Hassan's arrival.

"I telephoned the front desk of the hotel and asked about the possibilities after seeing your story broadcast in England." Jeremy chortled, "The name of the man who was a guest in the adjoining bedroom was John Smith. Hardly a name that would fit an Arab."

Virgo cut in, "I double-checked that, too. Smith - the most usual of aliases.But there's something else that could be a lead; I think Sirena, the whore, recognized the gunman.She must have seen him coming out of the room, and at first took him to be someone she liked.There was a frozen smile on her face, even though she'd thrown herself on Hassan to take the bullet."

I said, "A smile. Frozen. She must have moved very quickly, plunging to cover Hassan."

"Awful. He took the second bullet, and he's still in the hospital, although it was reported he'd only suffered a flesh wound."

"A lot of blood came out of him. Not nearly as much as poor Sirena, but still, a lot. I saw the two pools of blood when I was arrested and dragged to the crime scene."

Ellie said, "Jeremy and I have tried to book Hassan's suite. When we were told it was being re-decorated, and getting new carpet, we settled for the adjacent room. It's being readied as we speak. Meanwhile, we thought we'd take a look at yours."

Virgo gave me a sick smile. "In my other life I picked locks. Still comes in very handy for some of my assignments. I picked the lock to your adjacent room, Rick, I imagine Bokavitch will be roaring up here any minute, because we must be on the hotel's surveillance cameras."

"Cameras in the bedrooms? Maybe Hassan's, but surely not the hotel's!" I protested.

Jeremy agreed with Virgo. "Certainly, cameras in your suite. You're implicated in a murder. Better get back to your room and placate Bokavitch, while we have a look-see here."

I hurried back to my living room, just in time to open the door to a flustered Bokavitch. "What are you up to now? My security officer said there were blips on the camera."

I didn't dignify that by a reply. I offered him a seat and a tepid orange juice.

Bokavitch refused the orange juice. I guess he well knew what a classless brand it was. He issued warnings, "Our hotel, all hotels in Dubai, depend heavily on the tourist trade. If you screw up our business here, you'll be the next person to be murdered. Ha, ha. Joking, but not joking, if you know what I mean."

In the next room there were scurryings as if rats were busy inside. To make sure Bokavitch wouldn't hear the noises from next door, I turned up the TV before I ushered him out to the corridor. Good riddance.

After Bokavitch left, Jeremy pounced into my suite. He blared, "We've used Ellie's powder puff to put powder on the door jamb, knobs and even the toilet seat to check for fingerprints. None! this gunman was one hell of a professional."

Ellie joined him, with a long-faced Virgo. I thought that Virgo looked as despondent as a student who failed his A-levels, because there was nowhere to go with Happy's story.

I gave him the chance for a lead. "Let's go to the Emir Mohammed Hospital and call on Hassan."

142

16

At the hotel's entrance, we hired a taxi and Jeremy gave the address of the hospital.

Virgo pulled out his mobile. Before he could dial, I asked to borrow it and, after finding his number in my wallet, I called the groom who was tending to our two runners for the Dubai races.

"Jimbo, how are the two colts? Is Anchor favoring his leg?"

"Fine, Boss. They're fine, I had them out for gallops this morning. And no, Anchor isn't favoring the leg and he loves this hot dry climate. Uh, Boss, any word on Mrs. Harrow?

Jimbo might have asked for Happy before telling me about the horses, but after all he did ask if we had any news.

Virgo retrieved his mobile and dialed his office. "Can anyone there provide me with an interpreter? I need to have all that's been printed about Happy Harrow. Get onto Google for the print-outs in English."

So I learned that Virgo couldn't speak Arabic. How could he be helpful with no knowledge of the local lingo? He answered that with his first words, carefully using pig-Latin to confuse the driver who we suspected spoke English. Virgo said, "I'll use my mobile to call my M16 friend. He will be useful."

Virgo reached Forbes Paltry while he was still at my hotel, checking out the delivery area. Virgo snapped his mobile shut whispering, "Forbes will meet us at the hospital in the third floor waiting room."

Forbes knew the floor where Hassan was staying. He'd done his homework better than any of us.

We went straight to the third floor, where we found armed guards outside Hassan's door. No chance of entering there without some leverage. We went, as instructed, to the waiting room. It was full of women veiled with *yashmaks*, and wearing heavy cloaks despite the heat. No air conditioning in that waiting room.

And wait we did. Virgo didn't waste our time. He was on his mobile telephoning for a background check on Hassan using CNN's facilities as well as the newspaper where was employed previously.

When he finally shut his mobile, he wore an expression that promised news. "Apparently Hassan Massoud has interests other than training racehorses. I believe we'll get a few leads from these. A brokerage firm, for one. He defrauded a big client or two. One in particular who waited for his return to Dubai to shoot him here. Think about it. That could explain Sirena's 'frozen smile' for the man she recognized as he came out of the adjacent bedroom. Or, there might be something in the fact that Hassan bought a broken-down laboratory where he made over-the-counter cures. I don't know how that fits in, yet. And there's also a full-page on Google describing real estate scams he pulled all over the UAE. He sold non-existent houses, and apartments in developments that were never built, acreage located under water in the bay, or out in the desert with no water or electric improvements."

"Too clever by half," I murmured. "What about the surveillance tapes for the room adjacent to Hassan's? Sirena's killer must be on them."

"Blanked.We're dealing with a professional here. Someone who knows how to grease palms to get things done - he paid off the boys who file the tapes. Rick, you give tips here or you don't get anything. It's the way of life in this part of the world." Virgo shrugged. His expression softened as he watched the parade of comely nurses that swept by the waiting room.

Flocks of neatly uniformed nurses came and went. No *yashmaks* for them. This hospital had no scarcity of nurses,mostly fair-skinned blondes. I said, "I guess half these nurses are from England. Their educations were paid for by the British taxpayer, but they come to these countries for higher salaries. My father raged about this more than once."

Several nurses peered into Hassan's open doorway, then walked out gossiping about the CNN and the BBC TV coverage of Sirena's murder. they reminded me of nurses chatting in the *Godfather Two* scene when the gangster is about to be shot by a hitman.

Virgo started scribbling on his notepad. Ellie and Jeremy whispered to each other, their faces dark with anxiety. I was left out of those worries which were probably too dire for me to hear in their opinion.

Forbes Paltry arrived looking as expectant as a schoolboy about to receive a diploma. He said, in pig-Latin, "The delivery men who brought the rug to Mrs. Harrow's suite are on the hotel's surveillance tape. I've asked the local police to check for criminal records and mug shots of the two men. Now we're getting somewhere."

He approached the guards at the doorway of Hassan's room, and flashed a badge. Suddenly we were ushered beyond the open door and into Hassan's room.

Hassan sat up, in bed, a neat bandage covered his left shoulder. He welcomed us with a huge smile, "Praise Allah, you've come. It's wonderful to see you dear Rick, and Miss Eleanor. I've felt so alone. None of my owners have shown up to visit me."

I've never used a horsewhip, but if I had one I'd certainly have used it on Hassan - bandaged shoulder or not. I spat out, "Don't you 'dear Rick' me! Tell us where Happy's been taken, or I'll strangle you with my bare hands."

"No need to use that tone, Rick," he whimpered, dropping the 'dear' and ringing for a nurse. A sensational looking red-head appeared, with enormous breasts as fake as a Hollywood starlet's.

She slithered to Hassan's bedside in a style reminiscent of Sirena. Had she jerked him? Probably. they exchanged tender glances like a honeymooning couple. "You rang, Sir? More orange juice?"

I thought, "more something else." I said, "Hassan, you'd better forget your nurse and tell us where Happy is. My friend here, Forbes Paltry, was with M16. Any protectors you surround yourself with will be matched and bettered by Forbes whom I've ordered to put an end to you." An empty threat, but I felt I had to say it.

Hassan managed a weak retort. "I know Forbes. He works for a prince who sends me his discarded women - pal of mine, actually. As far as Happy is concerned, I'd like to be able to say I know where she's been taken, but I don't. I'd turned over the sale of that colt to Sirena. She was dealing directly with the owner, and you."

"Which colt? The picture she showed me in your Dubai hotel suite was of a ringer, and that horse was not remotely similar to the one in the photo I saw at Claridge's Hotel in London."

Virgo's cameraman entered the crowded room. Before Hassan could object, the camera's noise filled the space as it whirred and clicked. CNN was going to have the last word, and pictures. Virgo spoke into the mike: "You are seeing Hassan Massoud, who received the second bullet from a gun that killed his mistress, Sirena. He has just told CNN that the victim, Sirena, was involved in the sale of a colt - asking price in the millions, but Hassan switched the colts on Harrow."

When we had entered Hassan's room he'd had the TV on CNN. Now we saw ourselves,live, in the room on the screen. It was eerie. But it gave me an idea of how to reach out for help.

Hassan interrupted, screeching: "I didn't switch the colt. Rick Harrow claims that. But he hasn't seen the horse."

I spoke into the camera, nervous, but enunciating carefully, "I have no news of my wife, Hillary Harrow who has been missing for three days. She was abducted from our hotel. She is nine months pregnant. The kidnappers carried her out of the hotel rolled up in a rug. Please help us find her. If you have any information as to her whereabouts, please call CNN." I tried to control my voice, I didn't want to give a worldwide audience the impression I was a weakling. Steadying my tone and dropping it an octave, I said, "Yes, I had also been instructed by one of my owners to negotiate to buy a colt, but it certainly was not the one the late victim, Sirena, showed me in a faded photograph in Dubai."

The camera's noise stopped. Had I gone too far in using CNN to get help? Virgo looked anxious. He shoved the cameraman into the waiting room.

Jeremy Grace took up the gauntlet. "Hassan Massoud you're a dead duck if the gunman finds you here. All these pretty nurses won't be able to save you now that your location's been revealed on TV. Millions watch CNN. We won't need to deal with you; the gunman will. Tell us where Happy is, and we'll help spirit you out of the country to safety."

Hassan screeched louder. "Leave Dubai? Just days before race week! No! I've entered two horses in races they can win. Two million dollar purses, each race. I'll leave this hospital. Now! But not Dubai."

As he spoke Hassan was tearing at his bandage with his free hand. The bandage came off easily and revealed nothing more than a flesh wound. He lunged for a closet beside his bed. Then scrambled into clothes that had been hung inside.

Ellie, who'd remained silent,said, "You're not going to disappear on us. You're going to lead us to Happy."

"No! I'm out of the Mrs. Harrow thing. Nothing more to do with it. Forbes, take me to your employer, the prince. He has the best bodyguards and can put me up in one of his safe houses."

Hassan was attempting to pull up trousers on top of his hospital gown. He threw a jacket over his shoulders, grabbed his wallet out of the night table and strode toward the open door.

"Stay where you are," I thundered. "Maybe we will agree to let you hide at that prince's, but not until you give us some clues to help find my wife."

Hassan hesitated in the doorway. He grimaced.While he stood there a woman in a cloak and *yashmak* separated herself

150

from the huddle of waiting people and tried to pull Hassan into her arms. With bulbous eyes, she stared at Hassan from above the nose piece of her *yashmak*, then the woman made the Arab 'tongue yelping' voice of victory.

"Hassan's wife," Virgo whispered. "He manages to evade her most of the time, but she's latched on to him for sure right now. We'll have to include her in the little party we're arranging."

"No one leaves until Hassan agrees to give us some help."

"Rick, maybe he really doesn't know much. Sure, he tried to sell an overpriced thoroughbred to Hal Murphy, but there could be something we're missing here. How about if it was Sirena who made the switch. And she was killed to shut her up?"

"Sirena was no angel,we all know that. But what did she know about racehorses?"

"Whores can count money. She'd know the difference between a horse worth one million pounds and one worth three hundred. She'd have got a handsome cut out of that one million-pound deal."

Hassan was busily attempting to extricate himself from the enveloping embrace forced on him by his wife. Other cloaked and veiled women supported her claim on him; their yelps indistinguishable from hers.

Jeremy found the scene comical, and asked the CNN cameraman to take shots of it. "You can use this on a late-night reality TV show," he roared.

Virgo stopped the show. He pulled Hassan toward the hospital's elevator, repeating, "We'll get you to a safe house. The prince's, or another safe house nearby."

Hassan's wife followed and crowded into the elevator alongside Ellie, Jeremy, Virgo, his cameraman and Forbes. With the added weight of the huge form bundled into that *yashmak* and cloak, I wondered if we'd crash. We didn't.

On the ground floor the elevator's doors opened to a push of police,newsmen and photographers.

The media people had a field day snapping and interviewing Hassan and me together. For them it was like a nativity play where each of the reporters played the Virgin Mary.

I was past caring.

Where was the loadstone I'd hoped to get from Hassan?

We divided our group into two cars - Hassan went with Forbes. We tailed them to a magnificent palace on the outskirts of the city. It looked like a modern architect's version of an ancient prince's castle. If King Ludwig of Bavaria, in his day, had a penchant for old-style castles, why couldn't a present-day Arab prince live in a castle inspired by a citadel like Saladin's? With all his oil money here, he could.

Forbes steered past two guardhouses, showed his pass, and swept inside a fortress-like acreage dotted with large cement pillboxes set unevenly in order to deter terrorist attacks.

We lurked in our car parked beside a parched and dying palm tree.

When Forbes emerged alone ten minutes later, he was grinning like a student who had passed his O-levels. His car slowed down next to ours. He lowered his window and I felt a blast of over-active air conditioning. "He talked!" Forbes crowed. "He told me Sirena had sold out to a Welshman she'd met at the races in England."

"Happy, tell me what you learned about Happy's whereabouts."

152

"I'm getting to that. According to Hassan, Sirena was a double dealer. She'd ratted on him, and had also played the Welshman for a fool. He didn't miss; he meant to shoot Sirena. It was Hassan he didn't intend to shoot. He needs Hassan to complete the deal with Hal Murphy. Happy's the bait to make you agree to take the worthless switched horse."

"How does that help us find her?"

"He gave me the name of the Welshman - Jones."

"In Heathfield-accent English, from behind her *yashmak*, Hassan's wife's voice creaked, "Thomas Jones. Nasty piece of work. I warned Hassan not to have anything to do with the likes of him."

I groaned, "Thomas Jones. There must be a thousand Thomas Jones's in the world." I turned toward that mountainous woman, and without lifting her veil, said: "Do you know where this Jones fellow lives?"

"That one never stays in any one place for very long. He probably doesn't sleep in the same house two nights in succession. But we did get a card from him for a dinner party to be held in an apartment on Ayatollah Road. But that was four months ago, before the racing season. He goes to England for the flat races."

"Why are you telling us this? Why are you helping me?"

"I belong to the wives' club. And you are missing a wife." A pudgy hand emerged from inside the cloak. She waved it like a conductor's baton: "My name is Nelia. I'm the discarded wife."

"Can you lead us to Ayatollah Road?"

"Certainly. That's my intention. There's no guarantee Jones will still be there. I could almost swear he won't be, unless he has returned to one of his various stopovers. But I'd like to change cars. We're too crushed in this one. And I must go in the car with Miss Eleanor, because as I practice our traditional mores, I cannot be seen in a car alone with a man."

I finally felt a slight smile play on my lips. Who could even recognize this woman under her yashmak and cloak? I slid out of my seat to give her access to the near door, feeling relieved when she removed her enormous bulk. I'd been corralled on that side by her rolls of fat. No smell, no perfume or body odor, it was just her size that was so appalling.

Ellie jumped from her side of the car and joined Nelia. Forbes revved his motor and we had a difficult time to keep up. Virgo was not familiar with the streets.

We passed imposing white houses with sparkling red tile roofs, all placed in lush gardens crowned by palm trees. Leaving this area, we approached the high rise condominiums now so popular with English buyers. These monstrosities were extremely modern in style, most uglier than our hotel.

Night lights were switched on , and the boulevards glistened like diamond bracelets. One had an arch like a glittering tiara. Forbes stopped in front of the most luxurious building. A uniformed doorman emerged, followed by a security officer armed with a pistol on each hip.

"Jones? He left four months ago," the doorman spat out rudely. "No tips from that guy."

Forbes asked, "Did he leave a forwarding address?"

"Continental Aida Hotel."

Again Forbes revved his motor. We sped, in convoy, to the Continental Aida. There, we got the same story. "Try the Emerald Isle." We drove on to the Emerald Isle Apartments. No doorman there; just a row of metal boxes for mail, with no Jones among the names.

Nelia leaned out of the Forbes car and said, in that unnerving, tattered voice, "We've been looking in the wealthy neighborhoods. If he's down on his luck, which he often is, he might be among the foreign laborers in the trailer camps. Let's try there."

What a change off scene! From lush foliage to dusty roads and upturned garbage cans. We were in the 'slums' of Dubai - an oxymoron if ever there was one.

Rusting metal trailers stretched for what seemed miles along dirt trails that lead down to the highway. Far in the distance we could see lights of the dozens of container ships that brought in necessities and luxury goods and took out the UAE's few exports. Interesting how the newly arrived ships were lower in the water, whereas the ones ready to depart were riding high up. Lots of movement on those docks at this late hour, too.

I felt extreme pity for the poverty-laden residents of the trailers. They were walking like ants in long files up the dirt roads to their trailer hovels. Awful. Could Jones really be living in this miserable place?

There were no city services for the communities. We tried several languages on passersby, but no one understood us. Albanians, Estonians, Nigerians, non spoke English or Arabic. How did they perform their jobs? This was the manual laborers' world - language was unnecessary when carting loads on their backs like pack animals.

Nelia called out to a veiled woman who had a well-dressed infant. The woman spoke Arabic; she approached the car.

Forbes translated, "This woman comes from Darfur, she works as a prostitute. The child belongs to her pimp and is used as bait for perverts. Come on, let's get out of here. I'm going to be sick."

Nelia and I changed cars. I went with Forbes; Ellie and Nelia with Virgo.

I've always heard that women are the prime gossipers, but I personally believe that men can top them. Forbes soon began to prove me right. He tore into Nelia, "That awful old cow. she told me she is from a rich Saudi family, was sent to Heathfield School in England to learn to be independent by a mother who hated Muslim customs. What happened? Nelia turned into a fundamentalist - a fervent Muslim. She hated the London parties with the 'young bloods' getting very drunk and doing drugs. At the Regents Park Mosque she met some women from Afghanistan, Egypt, and Turkey who had renounced their new freedoms and returned to the old traditions. She joined their movement. When she returned to her disappointed mother, she was promptly married off to Hassan - a family arrangement."

"What did she have to say about Sirena?"

"Plenty. She'd known Sirena was his mistress, for years. At first she pitied Sirena, having to put up with Hassan. But then she was glad not to have to share her bed with Hassan. She learned that Sirena came from a poverty-stricken village near Turkey's tourist attraction, Cappadocia. Sirena got herself hired to wait on tourists by that balloonist and raconteur, Buddy Bombard, who carries tourists in his balloons over the sights of France, Austria, Italy and Turkey. Soon she was trading favors for tips with the single male tourists. Then, she ended up in Rome, where she became the *maitresse en site* of a wealthy Saudi. After he tired of her, Sirena was passed on to his friends. By then she was no teenager, and passed the thirty mark. Hassan was her last."

"No. Not her last. What about Jones?"

156

"Oh, Jones. We'll find him. We'll find out about that soon enough." The car took on more speed.

Both cars returned to my hotel at the same time. Surprise! We hadn't needed to scrounge all over the port; a message from Thomas Jones lay neatly on a silver tray inside my door. It read: "See you at eight, here, downstairs bar. Come alone. No reporters. Jones."

Virgo huffed over the note but agreed to give me space to see Jones in privacy. The cameraman was sent back to the local studio. Jeremy and Forbes offered to tail me out of sight, and keep a close watch, in case another abduction might take place - this time the victim being me.

Ellie and Nelia settled in the bedroom formerly occupied by Sirena's killer. Was it Jones?

Alone in the corridor outside my suite, I stood at a window staring at the City of Dubai, waiting for the elevator to reach my floor. Beyond the window was a Gauguin-like medley of colors. One building, that stood vertically, was lavender. Neon painted another skyscraper orange. Many of the palm trees in this luxury area had lights placed at their bases to throw up rays of varied hues. Crazy place. I got into the elevator, alone.

Three strides across the lobby, down the circular staircase, and I was in the bar. I wondered, "What happens to drunks on this staircase?"

Jones was an easy mark. He had the look of many a racetrack tout I'd dealt with in the past. These guys spied on trainers in order to sell information to bettors. Scum! He wore a loud checked jacket over plaid trousers. Dreadful. His shirt was the color of the neon lights outside - orange. His shoes were yellow plastic twisted with see through rope. Unbelievable. His face was the most arresting feature of his appearance: a large red nose, colored by broken veins, a handlebar mustache, and unforgettable piggish-pink eyes. Oddly contrasting with this unattractive picture were his hands - almost beautiful, elegant, like a woman's, with long tapering fingers.

"I've got a car outside. Come on, we're going to see the horse."

Which horse? He didn't specify. But now I didn't care. If it was the one that would effect Happy's release, I would have gone with him to Antarctica.

In silence we climbed the circular staircase. Where were Jeremy and Virgo? They had made themselves truly invisible. Feeling the hairs on the back of my neck, and against my better judgement, I climbed into a rental car of the standard variety.

Jones knew the local roads. We sped along without exchanging a word. After passing the world's only seven-star hotel, and the foundations of what is to be the world's highest skyscraper, we headed in to open territory. Suddenly, ten minutes from the center of town, with no indication, we entered horse country. Soon, we arrived at the stables for horses shipped in for Dubai's big purse races next week.

A spurt of language from Jones was unexpected as a tsunami, "The Nad Al Sheba Racecourse is a left-handed dirt track. Tricky. It was first laid down in 1986, but had to be resurfaced in 1997 before the racing of the third Dubai World Cup. Don't ask me why. There are three chutes: a 2,000 meter, a one mile chute for the Group 1 race, and a three-quarter mile chute. It's got a hard dirt base with seven inches on the surface which is fastidiously groomed and watered to keep it constant. The track is well-drained. I believe it is ideal for the horse we've shipped from England, and I know Mr. Murphy will be pleased to buy him. He is a very, very fine colt."

"I'll look at it. But I think Hal Murphy would want a colt that runs on grass, not turf."

"This racecourse had a marvelous grass track, special Bermuda grass imported from the United States. The grass went in originally in 1995, but it's been top-dressed with Irish peat since then. A wonderful surface, has bounce, gives a good cushion. Your colt will love it."

"Not 'our colt' yet. I want to see papers on the colt, from Wetherby's - the '*non plus ultra*' of racing establishments - to check the breeding and the vet's report. I want to look in his eye."

"You will. That colt is here." The car came to an abrupt stop, skidded slightly, and we parked next to a stable. "Follow me." Yes, to Antarctica, if I was about to gain Happy's freedom.

The stable was well lit, and air-conditioned. Most of the horses were asleep. But the one we came to see I recognized immediately from the first picture shown me. This colt was very alert, and neighed loudly.

Jones pointed at the horse like a Lebanese rug trader selling a carpet. "He's worth one million. He could win $2 million in the Golden Shaheen race, or even the $6 million Dubai World Cup."

"A tall order!"

"Remember how the actor Bing Crosby bought a piece of Meadowcourt the night before he raced and the next day took his share of a big prize? Mr. Murphy could do the same."

I ventured into the colt's box. I patted him, tried some of Happy's soft-talk on him, and then tested his legs. They were fine. I looked him in the eye, he looked straight back at me. No hesitation, no dishonesty there. I ran my hands over his pelt - no ringworm. The colt was sound. But was he the same colt as the one registered with Wetherby's that I was shown at Claridge's?"

"Harrow, if you still think this colt's been switched, I've brought a magnifying glass and you can read the numbers tattooed inside his mouth. Check them out." He pressed the magnifying glass into my hand.

I didn't have that information with me so I noted down the numbers I saw for future reference. This was a fine colt, maybe not worth a million, but no donkey. If the tattoo numbers matched, and I could verify with Wetherby's as to his breeding, I could legitimately offer to negotiate his purchase for Hal Murphy without shame.

"So Jones, why was I shown a different horse by Sirena? You must have known I'd never buy that mangy creature."

"I had nothing to do with her dirty dealings. And I most certainly didn't kill Sirena. I've been sleeping with her for years. I don't know what Hassan or his bloody wife told you about me, but I'm a businessman out to make a profit on a horse. Nothing more."

"You know what happened to Sirena? You know where my wife is?"

"No, to both questions. I watched you on CNN when you were in Hassan's hospital room. Of course you're desperate to find your wife. Who wouldn't be? Except, perhaps, Hassan! No, seriously, I'll answer your questions to the best of my knowledge. I'd been urging Hassan to make the sale on this horse. Sirena heard the ins and outs of one deal. Someone, your guess as to the man is as good as mine, was told by Sirena there was a million dollar deal. He got the idea of abducting your wife, and getting you to accept a worthless nag for your rich owner. That way, they'd sidestep the police; no ransom, just a horse changing hands. Sirena had the picture of

160

that nag when Hassan entered the room unexpectedly. Sirena's partner was waiting in the adjoining suite, ready to take the money he thought Sirena would be getting from you. When he came through the suite's adjoining door, and saw that Sirena had nothing to give him, he shot to kill her, and his second shot hit Hassan by mistake. Your wife? As for your wife, she must be in one of the trailer camps."

My hopes sagged. Whether his version of events was true or not meant nothing to me. All I cared about now was to end this horror and retrieve my darling. But how? The note from her kidnapper had not been written by this racecourse wheeler-dealer. The kidnapper was a far more ignorant, and obviously dangerous person.

I couldn't stop to negotiate to buy this fine colt when Happy's life hung in the balance - a kidnapper who wanted to trade a nag for one million in exchange for her release. I was, as they say - between a rock and a very hard place. But the scales quickly tipped toward my wife.

I thought, "Happy, if I could only find you before you have to give birth. And it's any day now that our child would be born - in a trailer camp, or wherever."

17

Happy lay in a small hut that had no furnishings, other than the rug in which she'd been rolled up. She positioned her body on half of the rug and used the other half as a blanket. The nights grew cold after the torrid days. Cockroaches and one curious mouse plundered the crumbs of rice passed to her three times during each twenty-four hours. She'd tried to avoid sipping the filthy water that accompanied the rice, waiting instead for the mint tea that came at dawn and nightfall. A chamber pot was thrust through the doorway three times a day as well, and taken away at the next delivery.

She made friends with the mouse, using the same techniques she used on horses - soft words and an occasional pat on the pelt. Happy recalled the history of how Walt Disney started his career making friends with a mouse in his garret; he called that mouse Mickey. "I'll call you Mickey, too." she whispered.

Happy wasn't bothered by the swings in temperature. During the day she stripped. At night, she put her clothes back on.

There was a small opening high up in one wall to provide air. Two days into being sequestered, Happy saw a piece of fruit glide through the opening. She caught it with both hands before the fruit hit the venomous floor. After the fruit came a voice in broken English, "Fruit good. Eat. Have knife for to cut fruit. Use open door. Wait for night."

Anxiously, Happy watched the pink rays of the sunset streak across a farther wall. When night proved full darkness, she heard a scraping sound of metal on metal. Nothing happened. The lock didn't give. The noise passed upwards to the opposite side of her door, and went from scratching to pulling. A bolt slipped free from the door's top hinge. More pulling, another bolt popped out from the bottom hinge. The door creaked open on its far side.

Happy didn't wait for an invitation to slip through the doorway. On the other side stood an Arab woman offering her a full-body covering *burkha*. The woman motioned for Happy to put it on. She covered her now-filthy maternity dress with it, and found herself engulfed inside the smelly contraption with a grilled window of crisscrossed ribbon for her to view this new world.

Without a word, the woman gestured for Happy to follow. They took a dirt road for a mile, then plodded through the scrub of a field. At its far end, a round hut displayed one small gleam of light - the flickering glimmer from a television screen! Happy got her bearings. In the distance to her right she could see the glow of Dubai's lights. To the left was solid darkness and the desert.

When they entered the hut Happy found herself welcomed into a huddle of women. Not all were wearing *yashmaks* or *burkhas*. This was home for some of them, and with no men present they could show off their souk-bought clothing. One woman wore a bikini.

Happy's guide said, "My name Toona. American soldier, he teach me English." A blonde blue-eyed child rushed to

164

Toona, and Happy guessed that language lessons wasn't all that the American soldier had given Toona.

"May I eat more fruit?" Happy asked, staring at a cracked dish holding a melon. Toona didn't take the hint. She pulled the dish away and pushed Happy on to a pile of cushions.

"Sit!" she ordered Happy, in the tone of a dog handler. Happy obeyed. After a few minutes of listening to the women chatter among themselves, Happy decided she'd make a move toward the open doorway.

There she was stopped. Toona's friendly manner totally changed. From a dog handler, she became Simon Legree. "You no go!"

Happy understood. She thought, 'I've been sold down the river. This woman, Toona, must have seen my story on CNN and wants a cut of that one million dollar deal.'

Then, the woman wearing the bikini approached Happy. With professional ease she tapped Happy's huge bulge. She nodded knowingly, and moved her hands southward to where the baby now moved. Again, she nodded sagely.

Could she be a midwife?

She gabbed to the other women. They conferred.

There was much head shaking, and many opinions voiced. Happy guessed they were saying she was nearing her time, but she wasn't concerned. She'd felt the strong kicking within, and that was all she cared about for the moment. Her baby was alive, and hopefully well.

Suddenly all the women who weren't veiled, and the bikini-clad Arab, pulled on their *yashmaks* and full-body coverings. A man in a *burnoose* had appeared in the doorway. He'd arrived silently on a horse, and led a second nag by the reins.

He pointed to Happy. She leaned through the doorway to judge the nag.

Could she ride the miserable creature to make her escape? She could!

Happy watched the man as he paid Toona from a bag of coins. While Toona bargained for more of the coins, Happy didn't hesitate. She grabbed the reins, slung her girth upward onto the surprised nag and was gone, leaving behind the dark, forbidding Arabian desert.

She knew where to head - for the glowing lights of Dubai. She heard a faltering patter of hooves and Arab shouts behind her, but soon lost the paymaster. He couldn't hope to catch up to Happy. This was Happy's chance to escape, and all she'd ever learned as a jockey came to the fore. From the pathetic nag she drew a speed which its owner would never have believed possible.

The lights of Dubai grew ever closer.

Ten minutes from the city Happy recognized a very familiar smell. Horse manure! She heard horses neighing and slowed her mount to a walk. Stables!

A car was parked next to one of the farthest stable blocks. She dismounted and led her nag to listen for voices.

She heard mine! I was arguing with Jones. She didn't recognize the other voice, but heard it say, "One million dollars."

Happy wondered what was going on.

She wondered if she should make herself known. She hadn't discarded the *burkha*. It was a prison, but also a protective shield. Her brief chance to watch television in the hut had convinced her that the was still somehow a target. What did she do?"

166

My darling wife gave out a 'mountaineer hoot and holler,' like only she could.

I'd heard it often enough at Paw's farm in Kentucky, and at races after a big win. I certainly knew her yell when I heard it, and I knew damn well there weren't many other Kentucky mountain girls in Dubai.

Rushing outside beyond the stable walls, I saw a lumpish figure in a *burkha*. She was tying up a nag that now looked close to death. This nag was even more loutish than the switched one Sirena had tried to sell me. It was a pauper's worst mode of transportation.

"Happy?"

"Rick!"

"My darling, are you... Are you okay? ...Our baby...?"

"I sure am now, but Rick, what's goin' on?"

"Don't worry about that. We've got a car. I'm taking you to the airport. Now. As you are, in that *burkha*! I've got to get you back to England for the birth."

"No, Rick. Not the airport. A hospital. Nearest hospital, hurry! My water just broke!"

Jones heard Happy. Exiting the stable at that moment, he rushed over, took her arm through the *burkha*, and led her to his car. "I know a clinic where they take the injured jockeys. It's only minutes from here." he said. Together we helped her remove the *burkha*. What a joy to see her face! I took Happy in my arms and tenderly laid her down on the back seat.

She gasped, "Labor pains! It's better if I sit up." She pulled herself erect. The car bounced along. After a very short distance we arrived at a futuristic building - the Nad Al Sheba racecourse clinic. We unloaded Happy, she grimacing from advancing pains. There was no doctor on duty, and no emergency station except during the day at race times. One solitary orderly was in charge of everything.

He couldn't speak English. Jones knew one word in Arabic: "Ingere," meaning 'hurry.'

The orderly shrugged. He pointed to a sign in three languages, including English. It read: "Doctors will be on call during race week."

I saw two uniformed nurses pouring coffee and gossiping. "Do you speak English?"

"Nein."

The second nurse snapped, "Non, not good. But I comprehend, when speak slowly you."

She stared at Happy's huge belly and Happy's facial expressions showing waves of pain. That told this nurse all she needed to know. She yelled in Arabic for a gurney, and Happy was wheeled into an operating theatre.

I asked Jones, "Can I borrow your cell phone? I must call my friends." I pulled out the bar bill for the number and dialed the hotel. I asked for my suite.

Jeremy answered quickly. "That you, Rick? Any news? Was Jones lethal?"

"Jones was...and is...okay. Colt's great but I still don't think I can buy it. The big news is that Happy's here with me! She got away from two sets of abductors. Rode horseback to the racecourse stables, where Jones took me to see the colt."

"What can we do to help?"

"We're at the hospital near the racecourse, but nobody here speaks English. Happy's gone into labor, and there's no doctor here, let alone an obstetrician. For God's sake, get over here. But first ask the hotel doctor to send an obstetrician to this hospital ASAP!"

"Will do. What else?"

168

"Bring Ellie! Happy needs a woman friend with her. And tell Virgo, give him the scoop, but he's not to publicize the name of this hospital. We can't deal with reporters or cameramen in this situation."

The hotel extension clicked. My instructions had been overheard. Listening in to guests' calls was as customary as snooping on them with surveillance tapes. For once, I thought, 'Hallelujah. My message to the hotel medic will bet passed on faster.'

I returned the cell phone to Jones. He looked jumpy, like a boy who needs to go to the bathroom and there wasn't one available. He must have overhead me say that I couldn't buy the colt at the moment.

Jones huffed out of the hospital, climbed into his car and left without a goodbye or a good luck.

The French-speaking nurse was gesturing for me to come into the operating room. She handed me an ankle-length gown, a shower cap to cover my hair, and two more shower caps for my shoes. At least this place was kept sterile. God knows I didn't want my Happy to get sick now.

Happy looked fairly cheerful. She was between labor twitches. Then, another big labor pain pierced her tranquility. "Rick! Tell me one of your racing stories to get me through it," she pleaded. "A racing story! Now! And make it one that I haven't already heard!"

I thought for a few minutes. Happy was struggling with tears, taking deep breaths and trying not to be a sissy. I began with a familiar personality, one whom I'd already spun a few tales about.

"Sonny Whitney really loved horses. And what he loved best was breeding them. He visited the foaling barns with such eagerness, you'd have thought he was a girl on her way to a dance. He studied bloodlines and race results, talked at length to the stable lads and gleaned information from jockeys who'd ridden his fillies. He was named 'a success in this field in spite of his wealth,' according to *Sports Illustrated*, 'a far cry from the typical rich American sportsman and socialite.' He adored Kentucky, and believed it was the greatest place on the planet to raise horses. He gave three reasons: "good bourbon, beautiful women, and not much else to do."

No comment from Happy. She was busy pushing, breathing hard, and gasping.

I continued, "Sonny Whitney's initial entry into the racehorse world was very successful, due to a horse bred by his father's Equipoise. But after the first four years, when he led the list of owners with top earnings, his luck failed him, and it was twenty-seven years before he headed that list again. Meanwhile, he'd been busy making movies, such as *Gone With the Wind*, heading up Pan American Airways, and Marineland on the California coast. In 1937 he announced his retirement from racing, but when he saw how many races were won by the well-bred horses he'd sold, in 1940 he got back into racing. But this time he hired an Englishman, named Ivor Balding, to help him with his polo ponies. This Englishman had a unique idea for turning around Sonny Whitney's losing streak. He suggested bringing a herd of Black Angus cattle onto his Kentucky farm to fertilize his acreage. Presto! Sonny Whitney's horses loved those pastures and began to win again. You might say, thanks to manure."

Looking at Happy, I realized she was beyond listening. The strained look had been replaced by fear and anxiety. "Somethin's wrong," she whispered, "I know it, I can feel it."

Behind me came hurried footsteps.

170

Robed and fitted out with the shower caps on his head and feet, Jeremy entered. He came accompanied by Ellie and Virgo. No cameraman, thank God. Not for this!

Jeremy spoke quickly in French to the nurse.

She nodded at what he said, looking relieved. "Dieu, merci!" she exclaimed fervently.

A small door that led to the washing-up area for surgeons opened. A man appeared. His gown and trousers were jade green. He had a rubber glove on each hand.

"This is Dr. Koprulu, an obstetrician," Jeremy announced. In a whisper, he added, "A Turk."

The doctor didn't waste time exchanging pleasantries with anyone. He examined Happy.

"Breech birth," he growled. "Backside first. I need to do a c-section. All you visitors please leave now. Only the husband can remain."

I stayed until Happy's blood flowed from the surgeon's deep cut, and I began to feel faint, when I rushed out into the corridor and then for the nearest bathroom, where I vomited.

Ellie was waiting with a cup of Arabian coffee to pad my stomach. We sat down together in an empty waiting room, Jeremy remaining standing by the operating room's door in case he needed to translate. Koprulu's use of English had been good, but what was a c-section?

Jeremy explained. "It means a cesarean birth."

Now I remembered that term. Happy had already had a cesarean section with our first child. Would it be safe to have this procedure a second time? "Oh, God." I felt so guilty, so remiss in exposing Happy to another pregnancy soon after her first just because I'd been so horny. I thought, 'God might forgive me, but would Happy?"

Although ashamed of myself, I had a niggling worry; when would we be able to have sex again if she *did* forgive me?

When the doctor emerged from the operating room, Jeremy spoke with the obstetrician. "Rick, the obstetrician has some good news for you," Jeremy translated for Dr. Koprulu. "You have a healthy daughter. And your wife is resting nicely."

"Ask the doctor if I can go in and see Happy."

Jeremy did. He said, "She's in the recovery room. Maybe you should wait a bit. But you can see your daughter."

I hesitated. It was Happy who'd wanted a daughter. I'd wanted another boy, a playmate for Tim. Someone we could play soccer with someday. "I suppose I must see her," I groaned, not really wanting to add this person to my family. This person who'd caused so much pain, fear and misery for my Happy.

The French nurse entered the waiting room with the baby bundled in a pink blanket. Her ugly, red face was half hidden by the folds of woven cotton. "Looks as though my new daughter - born in the UAE - has already adopted the *yashmak*," I commented, pulling back the blanket. Sticking out of the blanket was one tiny hand that looked like a boiled shrimp. As I watched, the little hand unfurled as five tiny prongs, fingers, took on the shape of a star. I placed my big paw in its way, and by God the fingers tightened on mine.

Bliss! Incomparable bliss! I bonded with that wizened red-faced creature far beyond anything I'd managed with Tim.

"Ugly little person," I murmured fondly.

Ellie objected, "She's beautiful!"

Virgo said, somewhat embarrassed, "Oh yeah, very cute. But Rick, we got serious talking to do. CNN viewers have sent literally thousands of e-mails congratulating you and Happy for the safe end of her odyssey. They don't know about the baby, yet. Rick, I need to tell this news to our viewers."

Ellie interrupted, "She needs a name. What are you going to call her?"

The first rosy light of dawn arrived as she spoke. Bleary-eyed we watched the many neon displays of Dubai fade and finally grow dim. I couldn't concentrate. I needed to see Happy. Desperately! But I didn't want to tire her.

The French nurse appeared. "Your wife, she is calling for you, Monsieur. And her friends."

We followed her as she led us down a short corridor. Happy lay with her knees raised holding a crystal-white sheet around her neck. The room was sanitized; no dirt here. She smiled wanly.

"My darling, my angel, have you seen our exquisite daughter?"

Happy's smile brightened. She didn't try to speak.

Ellie echoed my opinion, Yes, dear Happy. She's absolutely exquisite."

Jeremy coughed, "She needs a name."

Virgo said, "Yeah, please give some thought to a name for her."

I averted my eyes from my lovely daughter. "My mother's name was Hortensia."

A leaden silence followed that suggestion. Happy didn't even respond. After a few minutes' reflection, she whispered in a parched voice, "Dorothy. Like in the Wizard of Oz. We have tornadoes in Kentucky, and if our gal's there around the age of twelve, maybe she could look for the Wizard, and meet the Scarecrow and the Tin Man."

Simultaneously we visitors all broke into applause. "Dorothy it is. Hello, little Dorothy," I said, and chucked my daughter under her wrinkled red chin.

Happy's door opened. Fergus entered, sporting a huge grin making his full lips a wide crescent. "I think we're on to your man," he said to Happy. "A stupid Bedouin came to take the horse you left tied up at the stables and we followed him back to the hut where you were held. Lots of Arab women, most in *yashmaks*, and even a fatso in a bikini. All arrested by the Dubai police. That gladden your heart?"

Uninvited he sat on Happy's bed and gave a cascade of laugh.

Happy didn't join in. She looked grave, and saddened. "Greedy Arab woman, couldn't resist tryin' to make her fortune off me. But she has a little blonde girl with her. Just an infant. What will become of the child?"

Jeremy patted Happy's fluttering hand. "We'll look into this. Don't you worry your pretty head."

Ellie said, "And I've got a job for you, Happy, when you feel well enough to leave the hospital. I've discovered that in Dubai little boys, just five to eight years old, are used as jockeys in their camel races because they weigh less. They attach them to the camels with 'Velcro.' So they're prime targets. Thousands of these tiny children are forced to do this! You and I, we'll put a stop to it together. Our new mission."

A wan smile from Happy; she didn't follow up that idea. She said "I must stay here for another three or four days. Then I'm to see the doctor after a week to have the staples from my operation removed. Another week, and I can go back to England."

I leaned over the bed and kissed Happy. "You're going to be just fine. There's no hurry for us to leave now." I didn't

174

add that I wanted to further investigate Hassan's and Jones's involvement in the colt deal. Somewhere out in this overgrown city there was a mastermind who'd plotted the whole thing - to stick Murphy with a hopeless nag and use Happy as a trade. I wanted to find this Wizard, and track down his Tin Man and Scarecrow.

Fergus's mind was on the same subject. He said, "The *yashmak*-clad women in the hut may or may not lead us to the person who shot Sirena and ordered Happy's abduction. But they gave us two names which might be the men who carried Happy out of the hotel rolled up in the carpet."

I said, "I've stayed very quiet about the two horses I brought to race in Dubai, but I'm well aware they are racing here next week. We'll have time to get to the Wizard later."

Having a plan, I left the room and went to the hospital reception desk. There I encountered a woman who spoke up brightly in English. "May I be of help, Mr. Harrow?" Apparently, she was someone who had watched CNN. I hoped she wasn't going to tip off reporters as to Happy's location. I asked for a room next to Happy's. Not difficult. There were no other patients in the place.

When Ellie offered to stay and sit with Happy, I suggested that the male visitors accompany me to the stables so I could show them my two runners.

My real reason was that I wanted to discuss the possibility of finding the Wizard without Happy hearing what the chances were.

We found the stables where Feathers and Anchor were kept. They looked comfortable, and in peak condition. My groom had brought their favorite oats from England in cartons so there had been no change of food. They'd accepted the water because it was pure bottled Malvern.

They welcomed me like a good old friend.

After repeated nuzzlings and pattings, and carrots supplied by our groom, I tipped the groom for all his good work in the name of their owners. Then I cornered my three able cohorts. "All during the long and agonizing previous night, I wondered, "Who could possibly know about the one million deal.' I scoured my mind. Then I felt a slow realization warming in me like a winter fire. I recalled going up in the lift with Sirena at Claridge's, and how she insistently brought up the subject of the horse so that the elevator boy wouldn't take her for a call-girl. I tossed all this out to Forbes and Jeremy.

Jeremy agreed, "That's just the sort of leak that could have triggered this."

Forbes said, "Let me get on to my ex-colleagues at M16. I'm sure The Claridge's does a thorough check on all employees. Maybe even fingerprints them. I'll have M15 and M16 check those out. There are many international guests who could be targets for assassinations, so the hotel must take special precautions, such as background checks in its Human Resources department."

Virgo grunted, "He means, take precautions who they hire."

Forbes pulled out his mobile, "I'll phone Claridge's and ask them what their policy is."

We all listened on the speaker. Then a hotel switchboard operator came on, "I'll give you Public Relations," the girl's voice was loud and clear.

"No need," Forbes spoke quietly but distinctly. "Do you use temps? Are they fingerprinted?"

"I don't like to speak for the hotel's policy. You really should speak to our PR people. But no, no fingerprinting. And yes, we do hire some people on a temp basis when needed."

"Thank you. No I don't have to speak to your PR department." Forbes had a woebegone expression, like a fisherman who lost a prize catch. He said to us, "No luck there. But I'm flying to London tomorrow to bring back one of the Prince's wives. I'll drop in to Claridge's and ask around to see if any of the regular employees remembers a sleazy temp lift operator."

Virgo said, "On one of our programs recently we ran a story on DNA, and how there are new ways to track it. We could get some of his DNA off the elevator's buttons."

"And how do we find him, to get a match?"

I said, "We *will* find him, and put this whole horror to rest."

Forbes didn't leave. He added, "Rick, if you'd just buy that million dollar colt, that would stop the Wizard from trying anything else."

"I know. It's just that, for now, I can't check on the colt's action. I won't stick Hal Murphy with a good looking colt that has no speed, that can't or won't run. Hal's been a great owner for me. I wouldn't do it in any case, even to my worst owner."

"Telephone him. Nothing like a one-on-one dialogue." Forbes lent me his cell phone. I dialed Hal's Canadian number.

His wife answered the call. "Oh Rick, thank God you've called. We've been so worried about Happy. But we've just been watching CNN and seen she's back safely with you."

I added, "And had a lovely little girl, Dorothy."

"Was it a difficult birth?"

Women always want the particulars, I thought. I replied, "Breech, backside first. Happy had to have a c-section."

A sigh of sympathy came all the way from Canada. Mrs. Murphy said, "I'll get Hal."

The stentorian tones of my principal owner came through forcefully. "Good show, Rick. Great that you got Happy back safely. Is the story true that she used her skills as a jockey to escape?"

"Yes, Sir. You know what they say - once a jockey, always a jockey. Uh, I thought we should have a word regarding Anchor. I visited him today, and he looks in good form. I think we should run him."

Murphy was not to be put off the main subject. Are you going to buy that other colt for one million?"

"Mr. Murphy, Hal, you must know how much I want to buy him. But I can't drop you in it without proof. He may look good, great conformation and strong looking legs, big backside, but in all honesty, I should see the horse on his home ground to observe his action. He could be beautiful, but slow, or a no-trier."

"I didn't make my money scratching my belly, Rick. I'm a salesman, first and foremost. Believe me, if he's not as good as promised, we'll sell him on to some sucker. I don't have your scruples. I say buy him. I don't care if he's descended from one of the Arabians that bounded England's bloodlines, like Eclipse, Herod, Matchem, Darley, or Byerly Turk. Or the son of a Toronto pinto. I'll have my bank transfer the funds today. Plus another ten thousand for that nag the rogue has offered as a switch."

"Thank you. Thanks. Thanks so much." I would have kept repeating my thanks, but there was another call coming in for Forbes. I handed him the phone.

Virgo, laughing, said "I heard every word. That Hal Murphy, he's not only a clever merchant, he also knows the value of publicity. He must have guessed that CNN will give him all sorts of plaudits for tidying up this ordeal. That's worth far more than a million in PR."

A messenger approached Fergus, and handed him an 8 x 10 envelope. He removed the files, looked at a photograph, and murmured, "Hooray. Now we can get him!"

"What came?" Virgo prodded the papers. Always the reporter, he didn't miss a trick or a tip.

Jeremy said, "That looks like a driver's license picture."

"Exactly. I had my pals at M15 track the names of temp lift operators at Claridge's from the agency that supplies their temps. They had information on file that one of their temps sent to Claridge's owns a car, hence a driver's license photo. And his name is Harold Foyle."

I looked at the photograph. "Yes. That's the man who operated the lift the day I went up to Hal Murphy's suite with Sirena."

Virgo yelped, "What are we waiting for? Let's go get him."

Fergus said, "Let me borrow a helicopter from the prince. He's got three. We'll visit trailer camp after trailer camp until we nail this rogue you call the Wizard."

I agreed to the plan. But first I wanted to see how Happy was getting along. We returned to the hospital, and when I entered her room, Happy was sitting up, breast feeding our daughter.

Ellie was still haranguing her to join a crusade against using small boys as camel racing jockeys. "You must help. You understand the job. You've been a jockey. Happy. You must do your bit. I simply won't hear any arguments.

Happy smiled politely, but I know that smile, and it usually means "no." she gave me a brief kiss, definitely not one inviting sex, and said, "Rick, how did your runners look? any chance they could win here?"

"God, I hope so. Hal Murphy has just told me to buy both horses - the good colt, and the flea-bitten nag. I need to win for him with Anchor. And I want to win for Captain Ainsley, too, because it was really kind of Mrs. Ainsley to stay with Mrs. Roe and supervise the care of Tim. Feathers is rather an unknown quantity right now, but let's hope he has the qualities to win here. Doubtful, but possible."

"You all look like you're about to go somewhere..."

"Yes. The four of us are using the prince's helicopter to check out the trailer camps."

"My darling be careful. There's three of us to support now."

I kissed Happy, again no response to my need for sex. I added a warm goodbye to Ellie.

We went in Virgo's rented Land Rover to the prince's house, collected a much thinner Hassan, and took off in the helicopter.

"Shit, this town looks like Las Vegas, " Virgo grunted from above the tile roofs. We had a couple close calls with skyscrapers, but found our locations easily.

No luck at the first trailer's site. No luck at the second. At both places we'd shown the photo.

At the third site we struck gold. The man in that photo was strolling down a dirt path like a honeymooner on his way to meet his bride. When he saw us, he tried to run away but it was too late. Unheeding of other passersby, Fergus took a shot at him with his security guard's pistol, and the man promptly threw himself to the ground with arms outstretched shouting "mercy," in English, with a pronounced Welsh accent.

180

We dragged him into the helicopter. No sign of recognition from Hassan.

I asked the man, "Foyle, did you shoot Sirena?"

No answer.

Fergus put his gun to the man's head. "Harold Foyle, did you shoot Sirena?"

No verbal reply, but he nodded.

"Why?"

"Double crossing bitch. She wanted all the money for herself as a retirement from whoring - a nest egg. Ha!"

"And Hassan?"

"Put the fear of God into him...Asshole."

"Jones?"

"He's from my home village. But I couldn't get any help from him. I decided to hire local boys. Assholes."

I asked, "Where's the nag?"

"Here. And if you want to make sure your wife don't get no more trouble, pay up."

"You're going to the police station. But before you do, I need the names of the big boys who paid your air fare and for your local 'assholes.' I'll pay $10,000."

No response from the thug, Foyle, but he burrowed into a sleazy jacket and pulled out a scrap of paper with two names. I pocketed it.

We circled until we spotted a police station with a helipad. Going down was a bit dicey, there were two other helicopters hovering.

Fergus managed nicely, and when the blades stopped whirling, we delivered Harold Foyle to the authorities, Fergus doing the translation and giving them the UK driver's license photo.

The police were well aware of Foyle's crime. They had obviously watched CNN, BBC, and Al Jazeera with their separate versions of Sirena's and Happy's dramas. I signed some papers in Arabic that Fergus assured me were safe enough.

Fergus offered to fly us back to my hotel.

Thanks, but no thanks. I asked the police to hail a cab for me and Jeremy. Virgo crowded into it too, and directed the driver to first take us to where he'd left his Land Rover.

Speaking low because we knew the taxi drivers spoke English and moonlighted as spies, Virgo said, "I'm going back to my office, and give them the scoop about Harold Foyle. And Rick, guess what! While you were signing papers, I called the office and they told me they've been swamped with e-mails from owners who want to transfer their horses to your yard."

"That should bring a smile to Happy's face."

"Will I see you at the races next week?"

"Damned, if you won't!"

Jeremy grinned. Virgo said, "And Happy?"

I think I can say for sure that it would take more than a c-section to keep her from the Dubai races and our two runners."

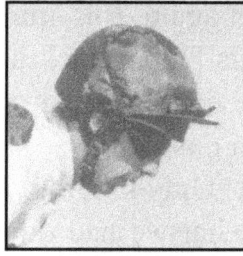

18

Last March 25 Dubai's $6 million Group 1 World Cup had been run. Now in early autumn we were in for big purses, but not anything quite that munificent.

Happy's equine concerns were for the health of our two runners, and what she could wear to the races to hide her still-swollen belly.

"Nothing fits," she wailed, once restored to our hotel suite with our new daughter. Cuddling Dorothy, she pulled out everything she'd packed for Dubai: "It's all wrinkled!"

I said, trying to calm her, "The hotel's valet service can take care of the wrinkles."

"Do they wear hats here, like Ascot?"

"Darling, I don't know. I'll ask Nelia. She wears the *yashmak* and sometimes the *burkha*, but although she'd hate to admit it, I'm sure she knows how to be cool in the latest fashion."

"Will she be going to the races, too?"

"Again, I don't know. I can't even guess how fundamentalists behave. But I'm damned certain that Hassan will be present. He's got two runners. And hell, if they aren't both in the same races as ours."

"He beat Arrow into second before."

"And he can do it again. But, mind you, his British-bred horses are as new to this Dubai track as ours are. And having been shot in the arm, he missed being present at gallops just as I was when you were in hospital."

"Sorry about that! Only kidding, it's my fault as much as yours. We both loved what we had done, and wanted another baby."

She kissed me, but still without passion. I changed Dorothy's diaper, not one of my favorite fatherhood tasks, and mulled over what I could do to beat Hassan's good horses.

And they were good. In the Group 2 for three-year-olds, Hassan took the race.

Feathers was the surprise winner of the Group 1 for two-year-olds. Having won at Lingfield, he wasn't a maiden. This was a race that separated the men from the boys.

I was so happy for Captain Ainsley. I knew he needed the prize money. He was still on active service and earning a decent income, but I had qualms about his future when he'd be living on the pittance of a retirement pension.

CNN covered the race, possibly because the interest in our abduction story had not waned. The BBC merely commentated on the main event for three-year-olds.

When the mike was passed to me by the CNN commentator, I said, "I hope to bring Feathers back for the $6 million Dubai World Cup in 2007. He ate up the track, and may do the same next year. Why not?"

"What about the Breeders Cup this year at Churchill Downs. Or will you be going to the Belmont autumn races instead?"

"I have another contender for one of those. I'm keeping him under wraps for the moment. So, don't expect me to give you his name."

"The exception that proves the rule," Ainsley said in reply, and cut short the conversation, ever mindful of costs whether from long-distance telephone calls or dinners in racetrack restaurants.

I felt good about Ainsley. I felt rotten about Anchor and Hal Murphy. After his magnanimous help, and I'd been able to do nothing for him or his horse.

But, in racing, we always feel there will be another time when the horse is right and the course's condition suits our animal on that day.

As soon as I could oversee the shipment home of our horses, Happy, Dorothy and I flew back to Heathrow. Mrs. Ainsley was particularly pleased to see us. She wanted to be reunited with her dogs and her husband. In spite of my winning a big purse for them, her first priority was home, dogs, then husband. I believe I'm right when I place them in that order.

Tim was not nearly as happy to be with us as Mrs. Roe was to leave us. He bawled loudly when he saw her packing suitcases to go visit her sister.

Tim had a problem with our lavishing affection on Dorothy. He must have felt jealous, because he began to glower at her and cry more often so that we would show sympathy for him.

I'd seen the same reaction in horses when a new star comes into the stable.

The next time he fell and skinned a knee on purpose, I explained that Dorothy was too little to take care of herself and she needed us right now. "We love both of you exactly the same. You're on your way to being a big strong man. You should help us take care of little Dorothy."

That didn't do the trick. Tim continued to feel like a second-class member of our family.

I was extremely busy down at the stables, and in the yard office. An avalanche of e-mails and letters had arrived; my office was too small for all the correspondence. There were blogs, and telegrams, too. Most of them congratulated Happy on her safe return and Dorothy. Some were hate mail. Environmentalists wrote: You are polluting the earth with racehorses. They eat our food and drink our water and are of no good to the human race. In case you hadn't noticed, they've been replaced by autos and trucks. The 'Save the Animals' group wrote: Whipping horses to make them run faster is as evil as whipping children.

I've never done either in my entire life.

Very important to my growing family's future were two letters from owners offering to transfer their horses to my yard.

The first letter was from Rodney Phillips, postmarked Edinburgh, stating that he had the perfect horse to win the Ayr Gold Cup. As I had already earmarked the Ayr Gold Cup for Anchor, I had to give that one a pass. I filed it in case Anchor's distance changed by next season, and that would be a good reason to court Mr. Phillips.

The second letter was from a tax evading Russian exile named Gregory Kotsky. He sounded promising. I knew that several enormously wealthy Russians were settling in Britain for tax reasons. I'd followed the pursuits of one of them, Mr.Abramovitch, who collected the Chelsea football team for himself, as well as other investments. Clever man!

So, I decided to give Mr. Kotsky a chance. I telephoned him, using the number on the top of his stationery. engraved British-style. "Da?" a velvet voice answered in musical tones.

Continuing in English, the woman said, "This is Irina. You want speak me or Gregory? He out."

"May I leave a message for Mr. Kotsky?"

"You wait. I push button for machine. Better you leave on machine." Her voice hardened, the machine clicked in, I relayed the fact that I was interested in meeting him and seeing his horses. Irina's voice came back on the wire, "*Oche harasho, our horses most good. Das ve danya.*"

That same day, after evening activities in the stables, the telephone rang. I heard Mr. Kotsky's pristine use of the English language. I thought, 'He must have studied elocution, too'

Mr. Kotsky had a large voice, a very large voice. He must have learned telephones when you had to shout in order to be heard over the eavesdroppers in his native Russia. "Kotsky, here. Mr. Harrow? Mr.Rick Harrow?"

"Yes, I'm here."

"Congratulations on the safe return of your wife. Irina and I watched the whole horror of it on CNN and the BBC. So you have my letter. My horses are very good, but I believe you could make them perform even better. Have you watched Tom Quelly, the apprentice who won 59 races in 2004? He could be as terrific as Lester Piggott when he joined Noel Murless in 1955. I moved to Britain in 2002, when the betting tax was eliminated. Great man, Winston Churchill, but he should not have introduced that betting tax in 1926."

I listened attentively, like a schoolboy in class with a new teacher. I didn't interrupt to say, "You certainly have memorized the important dates in British racing."

Or had he? Perhaps he simply had a book listing these facts and was simply reading them out.

He continued, "I have a colt related to Soviet Song. When can you come see him? You recall Soviet Song's great performance on June 21, 2006? My colt has almost the same breeding.

Good horse? Possibly a great horse? Would this colt offered by the unknown Mr. Kotsky win races for me? I doubted it. As in racing parlance: Lightening seldom strikes twice. Although if the breeding is close, there should be a damned good chance.

I said, "How about next Tuesday?"

"Excellent. I shall be at Longchamp in Paris at the Prix de l'Arc de Triomphe. October 2nd and 3rd. That will do me nicely. And you will meet my Irina."

I didn't wait for Tuesday. There was a slim hope that Broadback could win his race at Longchamp if the weather turned filthy. After all, he was a mudder. I'd entered him months ago, on the outside chance there would be a downpour for several days prior to the Saturday and Sunday races. The fees were steep, and I hated to pay them without some reliable meteorology report.

There were predictions for rain. I sent the horse by plane to Paris, where a friend and co-trainer who had offered me free stabling picked him up. Once I arrived, I stayed close to Broadback reveling in Chantilly's beauty. I loved the thatched-roof stables. Although,on occasions when they'd caught fire, valuable horse flesh had been destroyed. Meanwhile I brought my breeding books with me and I studies all I could learn about Soviet Song.

I needn't have bothered. Mr. Kotsky, whom I met on Saturday at Longchamp near the paddock in what is called the 'British section,' informed me, "My colt has the same ancestry as the magnificent six-year-old mare Soviet Song. I could send him to Fanshawe, who trains Soviet Song. Yes! But I became intrigued by your odyssey in Dubai. Therefore, in spite of

Fanshawe getting Soviet Song to a rating of 119 on the flat, I've chosen you. Yes!"

That sounded good. God knows I need more owners, especially wealthy ones. I'd check out this Russian's background to make sure he made his fortune honestly, and was not a member of some sinister 'Rusky' mob.

We stood together in Longchamp's superb paddock, admiring its tall trees that the Aga Khan and Duke of Devonshire's winners had walked under. Today's owners, like peacocks, showed off their fine feathers.Their ladies actually wore feathers in the Ascot-type hats over Paris couture clothes. But the rowdy Irish contingent of race viewers gave a carnival feel to the event. I looked beyond them to see if I could recognize any faces in this show-off crowd.

Damn! There was Hassan Massoud, preening himself, as usual. I hadn't seen his name listed as trainer of any of the runners on the Longchamp race card, but I assumed he just wanted to be a part of the show.

Like a homing pigeon, he came straight to my side, ogling Mr. Kotsky and waiting for an introduction. Hassan said, obliquely, "Dear, dear Rick.. You're always with the most fascinating people. This is the famous Mr. Kotsky, is it not? How do you do? And I am well again after that unfortunate shooting incident. All kinds of nice things have happened to me since then. I have two new owners. Rick, we three must dine together."

What a nerve! It was too obvious that he wanted to poach Mr. Kotsky for his yard. Famous Mr. Kotsky? No one had ever heard of him, not at least in the racing world.

"Sorry, Hassan, can't dine with you on this trip. I'm all booked up," I said.

Mr.Kotsky looked dismayed. I think he wanted to be one of a threesome to get in some socializing.

We did watch the Arc race together, enjoying the unequaled parade of great horses, and the victorious canter past the stands with their grinning winning jockey.

And we did become a threesome for dinner, but sans Hassan. Instead, Kotsky's Irina joined us in the Ritz Hotel's restaurant.

I never go to the Ritz without thinking of the footage I'd seen of Princess Diana and Dodi going through the revolving doors that was captured on the hotel's surveillance camera.

I studied Irina's hands. They were the most exquisite components of this most exquisite woman. She had the ice-blue eyes of women from St. Petersburg and the full flirtatious mouth of peasants from Siberia. The in-between bits were fabulous too - a full-breasted body and legs like an ostrich.

There was no wedding ring on either hand. I knew that in some countries the wives wore the wedding ring on the right rather than the left hand. Irina had no rings at all; in fact she wore very little 'bling.' Just an enormous diamond pin that shot rays of light, worn high on one shoulder, holding down a designer silk scarf.The other shoulder was bare.

Her destruction of the English language needed that diamond to equalize the shock.

No footsie play under the table like Sirena, and no hand working its way toward my important bits. But, at the end of dinner, when Mr. Kotsky excused himself for a late date, Irina turned to me. She said, "you like come upstairs with me my suite see my collections rare icons?"

Icons? That was a new one. I happen to like icons, whether from Russia, Macedonia or Turkey. I once visited a monastery in Turkey where the monks spent their entire lives painting replicas of ancient icons.

"Uh, thanks. I do think an icon collection must be a marvelous thing to have. Sure. Let's go and you show me your icons."

She didn't. She showed me her bed. When she'd left the living room, I'd imagined she'd gone to collect an icon or two that she kept in a safe. No. She reappeared in a black silk negligee, trimmed with lace, and worth the price of a yearling.

Unlike Sirena, she didn't present herself nude on the floor. She stripped in front of me, my important bits rising by the minute.

Sure, I love Happy. But, I also like sex. And I hadn't had any for months. Happy had been busy changing nappies, filling bottles for Dorothy or placating Tim. I hadn't gone without sex this long since before I met Happy, shortly after my live-in girlfriend of many years died of leukemia. I hadn't even asked Happy for sex until we married, because, being a Baptist, that's the way she wanted it.

Irina wasn't asking for anything, except lovemaking.

She smelled wonderful from Chanel Number Five. I simply couldn't resist - my manhood wouldn't allow it.

We had sex three times that evening, slept in each other's arms, and had even more daring sex three times in the morning.

I needed to go to Chantilly to oversee the shipping of poor Broadback back to Epsom. The horse hadn't been able to run because the weather had been wrong. He looked listless and frustrated. Believe it or not, racehorses suffered like any athlete that's stopped from performing.

I was back at the Ritz within a few hours.

Irina had left. Possibly because check-out time was noon and she couldn't afford to stay. Her diamond and expensive nightwear were obviously gifts. Her own expenditures probably didn't match up to her finances - as poor as her use of the English language.

When would I see her? I felt like an addict who had to have his fix. Would she answer the telephone at Kotsky's again? How else would I find her? I didn't even know her surname.

Everything made me think of sex - a doorknob, my umbrella's handle, the milk for my coffee reminded me of my semen.

I rushed to Charles de Gaulle Airport to the line of passengers waiting to embark for Gatwick. No Irina. There were trainers and owners, some gleeful at their wins,other frustrated from losing races. Jockeys preened if they'd won at the difficult Longchamp track.

Russian college students on their way to England to perfect their English language skills in order to get higher salaries, huddled together, practicing.

I approached the youngest of the boys and asked him to translate what Irina had whispered during our hours of sex. Never a word in broken English, everything in perfect Russian.

"Spaseve?" I asked.

"It means 'thank you.'"

"And 'ye vas lublu'?"

The boy looked shocked,as if I was some middle-aged pervert trying to seduce him.

"That is most passionate way to say 'I love you.'" He dashed away.

Bliss! Irina had whispered I love you. But why whisper? Why not come out with it?

I passed a Duty Free perfume shop. I suddenly felt so guilty I'd been unfaithful to Happy. I needed to ease my adulterous conscience.

I asked the salesgirl to suggest a scent for my wife. She sprayed Chanel Number Five on her wrist, and I thought I'd swoon from need of Irina. I bought a large bottle of Shalimar for Happy, I knew she liked that.

At the next shop I chose a plastic truck for Tim, and a cuddly doll for Dorothy. Somehow I felt guilty towards my children, too, as if I'd been a traitor to them, as well.

My flight was called. There was turbulence and I was told to buckle my seat belt. Constriction on my important bits gave me an erection. I really was in a terrible state.

Before I arrived on the outskirts of Epsom, I found a motel where I could shower. I'd showered in Irina's suite, but we'd had sex again afterwards. I knew I needed another good shower.

Happy was waiting at the door when I got home, with Dorothy on her hip and Tim holding her skirt. I waved, paid the taxi, and hoped she wouldn't read the guilty look on my face that could betray my shenanigans like how blood on his shoes points to a murderer.

I kissed Happy, and hugged Tim. I had all their gifts in a goody bag and proceeded to deliver them. Happy was delighted with hers. Tim pouted at the sight of his truck and said, "That for baby."

There was no Mrs. Roe. When Happy noticed me searching for her, she snapped, "Mrs. Roe has left us. Permanently."

Our house smelled of soiled diapers and sour milk. I couldn't help but recall how Hassan had warned me of the downside of domesticity when he first tried to get me to taste adultery. I felt a sudden urge to 'escape!'

Next morning I went to the stables. It was the time for our stallions to fulfill their duties and cover their scheduled mare. The head lad was preparing the mare with a heady potion to help her accept the stallion's advances. I couldn't watch the procedure. I was already horny, and still dreaming of my night with Irina.

From my office I dialed Mr. Kotsky's number. No answer. A message service trilled, "Please leave your name, the time of your call and a brief message." But it was not Irina's voice.

"Tuesday! I'll find her at Kotsky's on Tuesday," Went a refrain in my head.

I didn't. After alerting Kotsky that I was taking up his invitation to examine his foal, I drove to his stable and saw the horse. But no Irina, until lunch.

She suddenly appeared in the dining room. She ate quickly after a non-greeting.

No footsie under the table. No hand clutching mine.

I excused myself ostensibly to go to the bathroom and to write her a brief note with my telephone number on it.

To my consternation, she accepted my note, and went to a shredding machine in the office. I could hear its jaws eating my note.

Kotsky, not stupid, observed the performance. After she'd left the room permanently and vanished upstairs, he said, "You must overlook Irina's bad manners. Yes! You must understand that a woman so beautiful as Irina must have too many men making passes. She was afraid you were going to be one of those."

Over! Our affair was over. Already?

196

Pretending to have great interest in his foal, I tested its legs, looked into its eyes, and observed its action. He'd gelded the foal, I didn't know why. Maybe because Soviet Song was a mare, and he felt that horse without the 'entirety' of his maleness would be more successful?

"Nice looking. Good action. I'll be happy to take him to my yard." We shook on it. Hallelujah, now I had another owner.

Happy met me on our doorstep with sparks of light in her pupils. No infants in view. "Rick, let's go be naughty. Ellie's staying with the kids. I called a motel on the outskirts of Epsom. They're holding a room. Let's to there and make love all night!"

Thank God the motel she'd chosen wasn't the one where I'd gone the day before to clean up after Irina. This was a charming old manor house converted into a Bed and Breakfast with chintz curtains and flowered wallpaper to give the pretense of a honeymoon cottage. We took the bridal suite, and was it wonderful? Wonderful!

19

I felt it was imperative that I give Hal Murphy value for his money. I worked with Anchor every day, supervising his feed, his gallops and the rheumatic medicine for his favored leg. Several times I took him to the equine swimming pool for that leg. He took to swimming like a dolphin, up and down with the motion of a wave.

There were two final chances for Anchor to do his stuff before the end of the flat season - at Ascot on Saturday the Seventh of October, and at Belmont. There are two other great venues, one at Nakayama for the Japan Cup in November, and at Sha Tin for the Hong Kong Cup in December. But I felt the two last were just too far and the trip too costly to take a chance at either place. Like the Melbourne Cup in Australia, I'd never dared to aspire to go the distance.

Anchor loved Ascot. He'd eaten up the ground and sailed by his rivals there. However, the summer going is usually very different from the autumn. I read the meteorology predictions. I studied almanacs. I talked to some of the savvy old farmers in Berkshire. The weather report sounded hopeful.

I had another horse to score with for a rainy, muddy Ascot - Broadback - whose owner had stayed in my yard in spite of the disastrous weekend in Paris. No matter what the weather brought, my stable should produce a winner. If it didn't I knew I'd be in trouble during the long winter to come. Owners are phenomenally difficult to find, and I could easily lose my best two if their horses failed to earn their oats. I spent almost as much time on Broadback as Anchor, and gave him swimming lessons although he preferred mud to water.

At home my domestic life proceeded far better than what I deserved. Happy was restored to her usual high-powered libido. Tim had begun to feel protective toward Dorothy. and our little daughter began to demonstrate she had a character of her own by grasping at the Calder-shaped mobile suspended over her carriage.

Mrs. Roe had been replaced by a Mrs. Wright. Ellie had succeeded in enlisting her mother's most influential friends and relatives on her board for the foundation to save child jockeys in Dubai. Happy had embroiled herself in Ellie's project like a bee in a hive works for its queen.

With Ascot's final flat race day looming, I felt I'd done everything possible to prepare my two entries. All was well at home, I'd straightened out my love life,and there was enough cash in the yard's kitty to keep wolves from the door.

But, by late September everything went awry. One morning Tim was covered with spots. The pediatrician pronounced them German measles. We sent Dorothy with Mrs.Wright to Ellie's house to avoid the contagious disease.

Happy missed her period and I dreaded the news she was pregnant again so soon.

Burp gave his notice, because he'd been offered the post of assistant trainer in a far more important yard.

Our favorite jockeys were totally booked for every race and we struggled to find replacements. I was planning to run both horses, in their different races.Hal Murphy had advised me that he considered Anchor a great horse, able to handle any surface. And it was just about right for Broadback. Right enough,anyway, considering he wouldn't have many other chances in 2006. Both horses could possibly be kept for Doncaster's very late final race, but I hadn't done well there this year, and what's more, thought it unlucky for my stable. It was a long way to go from Epsom, and tiring to the horses. Both had thrived in the hot weather and might not run at the top of their form in freezing Doncaster.

My last day of Ascot for 2006 saved the worst for the afternoon. Both Broadback and Anchor came in second in their races. Always a no-no. Because first could have been only a nose away.

Later that day, I was summoned to the Stewards' office.I didn't think I'd committed any major fault; the horses hadn't bumped other contenders,the jockey hadn't whipped a rival accidentally. What did they want?

"We're sad to relay to you, Mr. Harrow, that your friend Lawrence van der Horn, died this morning in New York. We heard you'd intended to stable your horses with his for the Belmont races, and we've been informed that now that is impossible." A kind hand patted my shoulder in sympathy. The chief steward, a really nice man, treated me as if I'd lost a relation.

I had. Lawrence had been almost a brother to me ever since we raced against each other at Arlington, and I'd won in Chicago with Nile.

By not winning at Ascot, my little yard had less money instead of more. It was always costly to send horses to a course, pay the final fees,and give tips. How ever was I going to manage to take Anchor to Belmont, fly him over, and then find an affordable stable at that famously expensive racetrack?

Once back at Epsom, Hal Murphy came through with the necessities. I'd hardly had time to unbox the horses when the new assistant, Rex brought me an e-mail from Hal offering condolences for Lawrence and saying he'd pay all my expenses for Belmont, that I needn't put hand to pocket. What a wonderful owner, and friend!

Buy why had laurence died? I couldn't find out any details. He'd been in excellent health. We'd e-mailed each other to exchange dates for dinner at New York's finest restaurants.Cancelled,now. And would I make it to New York in time for his memorial service? Didn't know. Next day, I had to go into London to make arrangements for the trip.

Copies of the *New York Times* were always for sale at The Dorchester, so I stopped in and bought one on the day his obituary appeared. It gave the date of Lawrence's memorial service,and I marked it in my calendar. Very intelligently, the date chosen was on the eve of Belmont's races, which assured a large number of his associates would attend. Myself included.

The Dorchester brought back embarrassing memories of Sirena. What a mess I'd got into there. Thank God I'd turned down the invite to her suite.

I'd stayed loyal to my wife at that turn.

Happy wanted to go to New York. She'd liked Lawrence when we'd been together at Arlington. But I shied at the expense.

Another telephone call to Hal,and that was arranged. Happy must go too according to that kind man. No Tim, or Dorothy, though. The children were to stay with the new nanny-cum-housekeeper,with Ellie supervising when she wasn't promoting her foundation for the eradication of using child jockeys in camel races.

The scare of Happy's new pregnancy had passed. No baby this time. Happy hadn't been home to the US for many months and it would have been hard on her to cross the pond with morning sickness and fainting spells.

When we arrived at JFK Airport, Happy let out a Kentucky-girl 'hoot and holler' and headed for the 'Ole Kentucky' fast food stand there. She ate catfish, hushpuppies and grits until I thought she'd upchuck. I played escort,and remembered how I'd missed my malt whiskey and scones when I was away from England.

Hal had booked us into a hotel called the Carlyle, all expenses paid. Very grand and full of Aristos from both continents. There was a piano bar downstairs in the lobby. I left Happy sitting in bed, watching TV and devouring her room service vittels while I escaped to the bar.

The first person I saw was Hassan Massoud. I could hear his pompous fake Oxford tones booming over the piano and singer as I entered the bar. The second person I saw was my former trainer and boss, Bono. These two were as close as a bride and groom on their wedding night.

Though not intending to eavesdrop, I couldn't help but overhear Hassan wooing Bono.

Hassan complimented him on his handling of Nile and bringing him to the Belmont to compete in a mile race. I'd hoped to do that myself not too long ago, while I was still an assistant trainer to Bono in Los Angeles.

Bono seemed ultra-careful in responding to Hassan. This bride was flirting with her bridegroom but not yet quite ready to give up her flower. "We could talk about trading Nile, if my owner agrees," Bono told him half-heartedly,and obviously uncomfortable with Hassan's high-powered sales tactic.

Hassan saw me standing in the doorway and summoned me to join them at their table. He said, "Bono's giving me pointers about the American way of racing. Not too changed from when we were all at Arlington, but good to hear in any case." That certainly was not what they had been discussing, but I pretended it was, like the best man at a wedding who submits to joining in the event's good cheer,although his heart is being wrenched because he'd hoped to marry the bride himself.

It wasn't that I felt surprised to see Hassan here for the Belmont races. After all, his horse had beaten Anchor twice,once in England and again in France.

I was surprised, however, to hear him push Bono to give a lecture to various international guests on the fine points of American racing and race tracks. What was Hassan's motive? Hassan never made a move without a purpose.

He said, "Racing in America seems so different. Contenders go out fastest at the gate and keep up the pace until they get to the finish. We give our runners a breather. They don't. And the bends are so sharp.The tracks are left-handed. And whether you are talking Bermuda grass or the turf,they are kept far too firm.But the worst is that dope is allowed in many states - bute, and almost always lasix."

Bono contradicted him, "Not in New York State, where the Belmont Cups are run. And I've seen tracks that were puddles from one end to the other."

Hassan doesn't tolerate being contradicted. His full lips tightened. His eyes narrowed. But he maintained a smarmy smile. "I'm sure you're right and I'm wrong. Let's drink on that. Rick! Do you still drink malt whiskey? They have it at this bar."

204

My voice tight, I said, "Hassan I suppose you're running your two year olds here?"

"Most certainly, dear boy. And I've found a fantastic jockey. One who understands how two year olds are prone to wandering around a track. He'll keep mine steady. I assure you."

I thought, 'Because you'll cut off his balls if he doesn't.'

Bono said, "We've got over five hundred racecourses in this country, with thousands of apprentices and jockeys. How'd you find this wonder?"

"Advertised. The best way, of course."

"And how did you get this wonder away from his trainer?"

Hassan hedged, "Oh, the usual way."

Bono caught my amazed look and glanced away hoping Hassan noticed his own shock. "I hope you haven't poached mine." He immediately left the bar, probably going to check i\on which jockeys.

Hassan's smile widened for me, "Your old friend Bono has a very short temper."

Slightly supercilious, I changed the subject, saying, "And in which of the championship contests have you entered your colts?"

"All the same as you have, dear boy. Our runners are so evenly matched. I hope you treat me as fairly as you did Bono, just now. Agreeing with him all the way. And you have so many reasons to detest him after he grabbed our owner and Nile."

"I've got a headache," I said. "I'm going back up to my room to eat something. The food on our plane was disgusting."

"Here. Let me give you an aspirin. Just the thing for a headache!"

He advanced his oily palm holding a round, flat white pill. What did I remember about aspirins? Tired from the flight, I couldn't quite recall. But I shook my head and quipped, "Thanks, but no thanks. I'm just hungry. Food will do the trick."

I left Hassan cooing to another trainer and sucking up big time. I'd seen that act before.

No one I knew in the elevator.No one I knew in our corridor. Happy's welcoming greeting warmed my cockles. "Hi! Jump in bed with me. I want some loving." At last, no excuses, no baby bawling or diaper to change. Just Happy and me and a big bed! The race was on,and there were no horses in sight.

It was delicious! There's something about sex in a fancy hotel room that adds spice, like ginger to apple pie.

Later, Happy felt like chatting. Unusual,because customarily, after sex, she rolls over and goes to sleep.

"I hope you don't think bad of me 'cause I didn't bring the kids with us. I took Tim to Chicago when he was tiny, but remember, Princess Diana took Prince William to Australia when he could barely sit up. And she left both her children back in England for other trips."

Although Happy had been a mere nine years old when the Princess died, Diana was one of Happy's heroines. Happy had read a dozen books about Princess Diana. Happy added, "Too bad she didn't like to ride horses."

Listening to Happy talk about her heroines, I remembered how much she wanted to meet movie stars in Los Angeles. I'd seen one in the Carlyle's lobby.

"You want to meet a movie star? There's one in this hotel right now."

Happy was out of bed like a thoroughbred aiming for the finish line. She was dressed in seconds. I pulled on my cords and a sweater and we went downstairs, hoping the star would still be in the lobby.

She was.

Taking a good second look, I recognized her. She was Sybil Sykes, who usually played in comedies.Tall,too thin,too angular but with a fabulous face,the star had draped herself over the porter's desk.I heard her ask, "How do I get to Sotheby's from here? I was told it was within a few blocks."

"Within a few blocks. That's correct madame. Go out the front door and turn left."

"Call a limousine for me."

"Certainly madame. But it is only a few blocks."

"I said, a limousine. Now!"

Happy listened to this exchange, her face glowing as if I'd won the Arc race with a no-hoper. "She is gorgeous. I'm in heaven."

We stood beside her under a heated canopy pretending we were waiting for a limo, too. Happy's eyes glistened like tinsel on a lit Christmas tree. Then, she struck up a conversation, keeping her voice normal as if she chatted with movie stars every day. "Y'all goin' to the races tomorrow at Belmont?" A few Kentuckyisms slipped through.

Surprisingly, this acidic woman warmed immediately to Happy. "Well, I might go. Today and tomorrow are my free days, and I'm doing what I damn please. I'm fed up with having what *I* want fucked up by a wimpy producer. Tell me, kiddo, where are you from? What's that accent?"

Happy blushed. She hated being singled out because of her Kentucky country accent. Sighing, she told Sybil the truth, but this time laying on the accent with full force. "Ah'm jus'ta girl from the Kentucky mountains...A mountaineer!"

A limousine swerved up to the curb. The Carlyle's doorman gestured to Sybil that this was her transport. Sybil pushed Happy into the car. I had a hard time convincing the woman that I was Happy's husband and must come, too.

Then came a spate of verbage from Sybil. "Mountaineer! How wonderful. Just what I need. I'm contracted to play the female lead in a new movie about mountaineers, *Hogtown II*. And shit, I haven't a hope in hell of getting the accent right. So what are you doing the next two days? Can I hire you to coach me in that accent?"

Happy, noticing she'd forgotten to introduce herself, blurted, "Happy. Mrs. Rick Harrow,...and, yes!" Then, Happy's face broke into her wide crescent grin. "Y'all wonna' talk lake a mountaineer...Ah'll show ya how! But Ah's all tied up tamarra'. Ma husban', Rick, he's a racehaws traina', has a runner at Belmont tamarra'."

Sybil and Happy hugged like long lost mountain 'cuzints.'

Sybil finally acknowledged my presence in her limo. "I want a racehorse, Rick. Maybe two or three, which will give me a better chance to win one of those fucking races. LA's Santa Anita track owes me money because I've lost so many bets there. I'd give anything to win it all back from them with some fucking horses of my own. Tell me about it; what do I need to do to get a horse? How much does it cost?"

Two or three horses! I felt like telling Happy to move over and give me her space in heaven.

I said, "I train in England because having horses in England isn't as expensive as here. You'd have to bid against owners from other countries to get the finest horse flesh, just as

208

you would no matter where you train, and that could cost anywhere from $17,000 for one of the greatest horses ever, Seattle Slew, to $6 million, that some of the Arabs are paying these days."

"I can afford whatever I fucking want. I made $20 million last year on two movies!" Sybil saw the Sotheby's sign and yelled at the limo driver to pull over. She sidled out onto the curb. "How should I say that to the driver? Y'all curb this truck?"

Happy, prancing like a trotter next to her new friend, shook her head and said, "Mista' tha'd be fah'n rat here. We all needs some hushpuppies, so stop this here ve'hick-l ova heah." Thank God Happy didn't follow her dialogue with a usual holler.

Sybil listened with intense care. She was no amateur; she knew her business. "I want you to read the script they sent to me and correct it so I can make it authentic. And then teach me how to pronounce what's fucking right, instead of the writer's phoney attempt."

Happy answered, "Ah who-nuf will!"

We entered Sotheby's as a threesome. And wouldn't you know my luck, it was the day for the Russian icons auction. I thought of Irina, but my penis didn't grow hard. What the hell, I hadn't even grown hard in the limo as I sat next to gorgeous, famous Sybil! Happy had taken care of me in that department.

Sybil placed a bid on two icons, a superb eighteenth century one with a vermeil gold-topped cover, and another seventeenth century faded beauty. Happy drew us away to an exhibit in the next room. It was of Arab art.

"Look at that." She pointed out a brass coffee pot encrusted in gold.

Sybil didn't respond. Sybil was busy trying to buy these items right out of their case.

A Sotheby's flunky came over and explained, "Madame, these articles are listed for auction. You have to bid on them."

Sybil engaged her shoulders in a well-known jiggle she'd used in her last three blockbusters and stalked off.

In her dash to get away from the flunky who outright insinuated she was an ignoramus who didn't know it was necessary to bid at Sotheby's, she collided with a cowboy. The man was Sol Jones, the owner of Nile, and my friend - at least before the Bono ordeal.

He wanted everyone in Manhattan to figure him as a rich Texan. He wore a ten-gallon hat, high-heeled embossed leather boots, and a string tie. He could have walked right on to the set of *Dallas*. But 'I knew him when,' as the saying goes.

He recognized Sybil as the star of *Hogtown*. That film had bombed because Sybil had played the heroine in the style of a hooker instead of a Kentucky mountain girl.

That was the mistake she intended to repair in *Hogtown II* by plumbing Happy for character tips and imitating her accent.

"Whoopee! If I ain't been bumped by Miss Hogtown herself. How about meetin' me for a glass of bourbon?"

Sybil snorted, "Well, ain't you a cute one. And Ah sho' won't say no ta' that!" Sybil couldn't resist practicing her part at every chance.

Sol came accompanied by an abashed looking Bono. He was pleased enough to play sidekick to an overacting Texan when in Hollywood, but in Manhattan Sol was an embarrassment in his bad taste Texas get up.

But he was one embarrassment I wouldn't back away from. God knows how I'd love to have Sol and Nile in my yard.

210

I said, "Hi, Sol. Good to see you. Hello Bono, why'd you leave me stuck with Hassan in the bar?"

Bono shrugged. He grimaced, and looked as if he would spit tobacco juice if he'd been a chewer.

And, speaking of the devil, Hassan appeared at that moment as we were checking out the Arab art.

He sucked up to Sol, ignored Bono and me, and omitted any respect for Happy or for our famous movie star friend.

Sybil said kindly, "Come on, kiddo. We don't need to be snubbed by the likes of that character. Let's get the limo. You can bring your husband and the Texan, too. The four of us can go out on the town."

Hassan wasn't that easy to discard; like a tick that burrows into your skin, he said, "I can get us into all the best places." Sybil had to break down and let him join our little gang.

When Sybil's limo reappeared on demand, we all crowded into it and opened its bar. This was a stretch limo, caparisoned with an assortment of bottles and tidbits.

The driver, ordered to take us to "21" and then to the Four Seasons, swung the long frame of his vehicle around the crowded corners of Manhattan's most classy district.

Swaying, and drinking unfamiliar booze, Happy turned pale. "I think I'm going to be sick."

Hassan was quick to offer her a bottle of his small, round flat white pills. "Here, dear little lady. Take a couple of these. Best aspirins in the world."

"Uh, thanks. I'll take one for later. I simply wouldn't be able to keep it down right now."

Bono said gruffly, "Give me some of those. My head's killing me." He took the whole bottle of aspirin off Hassan, and downed a few there in the limo with the help of straight bourbon.

"Glad to help you out." Hassan boomed in his fake Oxford bellow. "And driver, I wish to get out at the next corner."

Hassan left us, and quickly I collected his aspirin tablet from Happy. "Let me have that," I said. "We'll get you an Alka Seltzer at the hotel.

At the Carlyle, Sybil gave us a fond 'too-de-loo" and disappeared with Sol toward her suite.

Happy commented, "No nice Baptist mountain gal would take a stranger up to her room like that. But, then, she's only pretendin' to be one in her movie. That's Hollywood."

I hurried Happy to our bathroom. "Take a shower. Let the water play over your face. Forget the aspirin."

20

The next morning we collected Sybil and went in her limo to Belmont. I took both women to see the horse boxes, and introduced Sybil to our two runners, Anchor and Feathers. Sybil was duly impressed and wanted to buy them away from their owners on the spot.

Rather pompously, I said, "I'm loyal to my owners. And the owners of these two runners have been particularly kind to me."

I read the race card to study the competition. I hadn't had time to read the line-up in the morning newspaper; it had been enough to listen to the weather forecast on our TV.

Hassan's two winners were still in. Nile was entered in the 10-furlong Jockey Club Gold Cup, worth $75,000. I felt so proud of him, and a little in awe of Bono to have re-trained him to that distance. Anchor was in the Vosburgh for three-year-olds and up, with a prize worth $400,000. Feathers we'd have to wait to see him run in the Champagne Stakes for two-year-olds - over a mile, worth $400,000. All of my horses were down for Grade I events. Rather cheeky of me, I'll admit. But if you don't enter them you can't win.

I checked out the winners in 2005. The Taste of Paradise, trained by Gary Mandella with Garrett Gomez in the saddle, had won the big one.

The going was perfect for my string. They were in the best condition possible, even after their long flight across the pond. And I liked our jockey.

Anchor won easily. Hassan's entry didn't leave the gate fast enough. Poor sportsmanship on my part, perhaps, but I was delighted to have bested him this once.

Happy, Sybil and I were quaffing victor's champagne, when a dreaded summons to the Stewards' office came for me.

'Please, God,' I thought, 'don't let them take away our win. It will mean so much to Hal Murphy, and he deserves it.'

Long faces, no pats on the back in the Stewards' office. What had I done wrong?

Belmont's stewards have different jurisdictions: Carmine Donofrio representing Belmont; Dr. Theodore Hill representing the Jockey Club; and Braulio Baeza acting for The New York Racing Association. These are serious racing men with great reputations.

What had I done wrong?

A secretary, speaking in solemn tones, said, "We're sorry to tell you that Mr. Bono Munoz died during the night and Nile won't be running. As you were the trainer who originally prepared Nile, we thought you should be informed privately rather than simply learn it from the announcement at the race track."

The news hit me hard, like when you're shoveling snow and you strike a rock. Munoz!

He was fine yesterday at Sotheby's.

No, not fine in the limo. He said he had a headache and needed an aspirin.

Aspirin, again! Ever since our first neighbor Josh Rawlence died from taking aspirin with his prescription medication, I've been haunted by those damn white pills. What the hell, there had to be an explanation, a tie-in?

Happy and Sol were in the Belmont's elegant Director's Room, surrounded by its magnificent collection of rare paintings featuring racing scenes. The two of them seemed so exhilarated after Anchor's win, and with equal anticipation for Nile's upcoming performance, they couldn't understand my obvious misery.

Sol asked, "Hi ya, old pal. Why the gloom? It just ain't appropriate on a day like this in a place so special-like."

Happy said nothing. She nodded her head in agreement with Sol, but Happy knew me better and guessed something terrible had happened.

"What is it?" she murmured, placing a comforting arm across my back.

"Bono Munoz. Dead! He wasn't my favorite person. I worked for him because I had to support my family. He dealt me a dirty deal with Nile, yet I'm horrified that he went so quickly. I've been to the Stewards. Same story as in the Directors' Room ad Lingfield, and as at Ascot. Same cause of death, too."

"What was the cause?"

"Heart attack. He was only thirty-eight years old. I never noticed any symptoms of a heart problem when we worked the horses in his yard. He galloped hard and jumped out of the saddle like an acrobat!"

Sol was now concerned over how this was going to affect Nile. "Gawd almighty, my horse cain't run! Not until his assistant trainer gets all the paperwork done."

Hassan pushed his way into the Director's Room. He asked for a glass of juice, then joined us, uninvited.

"Mr. Jones, may I offer my condolences? I've just heard the news. And, incidentally, I'd also like to offer you my services as a trainer."

I thought, 'How tasteless. And what gall!'

Happy bridled, "Hassan Massoud! You should be ashamed of yourself. Bono isn't even buried, and you come here to scoop up his owner. I call that disgusting."

Hassan bared his teeth in a forced smile. "Dear little lady, I know you have no idea of what you are saying, so I will overlook that remark."

But he retreated from the Directors' Room. Happy had made him turn tail.

Sol went into a funk, cocking his hands to his forehead like a monk in deep prayer. After a long pause, Sol lifted his drink and toasted Bono. "To a not-very-good man. I liked you for the fast cars you bought for me, but I despised you for the dirty tricks you played on my friend, Rick. And, now, Rick, tell me; what am I to do about Nile?"

"You have to follow the correct procedures on this, Sol. It's complicated, but you have to do what's correct. Then I think you could run Nile at Churchill Downs on November 2nd, in the Breeders' Cup. He's good enough. I promise you, I bought that horse as a yearling and know him very well."

I wasn't hinting that I'd like to train him again. It wouldn't have been the gentlemanly thing to do. As Happy had emphasized, it was too soon. It would have been indelicate right now to propose myself in that capacity. Also, I needed to find the form for a British trainer to transfer a horse in training to his stable in time for the Breeders' Cup

216

race, three-year-olds and up; worth one million dollars. Crist-on-a-bike, my yard would earn one hundred thousand if Nile won. But I knew Bono's assistant trainer, now probably heading his yard, wouldn't be an easy man to dislodge.

We returned to the Carlyle in Sybil's limo, our spirits dampened even though Anchor had earned $400,000, of which $40,000 was headed toward my yard. Sybil was interested in learning about the child jockeys in Dubai and had not only offered to front the foundation's campaign, but said she'd go to Dubai and find a poster-child to feature; she knew the ins and outs of promotion.

There was an ominous note waiting for me in our room. It was from a Long Island coroner requesting my presence. Ouch! Not again! I'd been through this two years ago when the girl jockeys were killed in Saratoga.

In his bare office, under cruel fluorescent lighting, the coroner informed me that an autopsy was to be performed on Bono. His relatives in California had requested it.

"They think there's been foul play. And, strangely enough, I have an e-mail here from a Munoz cousin who suggested I also look into the recent death of Lawrence van der Holt, which he claims was similar. Another trainer. Friend of yours?"

"Absolutely. And a great trainer, and good man."

"We're looking into the possibility of a connection. Mrs. van der Holt has agreed to help us."

"Is his body going to be exhumed?"

"Van der Holt was cremated."

"How can she help? In a way that a jury would accept?"

"There are very sophisticated methods of testing for DNA available to us now. We'll extract samples from hair brushes, that sort of thing."

This coroner was quite a guy. I was duly impressed. I saw him again at the memorial service for Lawrence when he showed up for it - something I'd list as beyond the call of duty.

I watched him having a serious discussion with Mrs. van der Holt following the service, when the line of mourners had thinned. She looked more than unhappy; dismayed was a fairer description. Happy had waited until other friends had left to place her arms around the weeping widow.

Without meaning to eavesdrop, she'd heard the end of the dialogue between Mrs. van der Holt and the coroner.

He'd said, "Cyanide showed up in the hair samples."

Cyanide?

What a way to commit suicide, if that's what Lawrence had actually done!

But cyanide was used in the extraction of gold and silver; did Lawrence know any jewelers, or how would he have gotten the damn stuff any other way?

Depressed, Happy and I returned to our suite. This was to be our last night at the Carlyle, and glories of our trip to New York had vanished like the air let out of a tire.

Happy surprised me with an unexpected idea. "I'd like to stay here in the US, go to Arkansas, and check out what happened to Whitey. What really killed him. It seems too weird that both he and van der Holt, and now Bono, all died from heart attacks, only now we know in Lawrence's case it was cyanide."

Within minutes, while we were packing, the telephone rang. The voice in the earpiece was Hal's.

He said, "I've been thinking. Maybe you should keep Anchor on this side of the Atlantic and train him here. We could run him at Churchill Downs during the Belmont Cup meeting in November. How about it? Can you leave your kids that long?"

Happy had listened in on the extension in our bedroom. She came to the doorway and nodded affirmatively. "Tell him I'm willing to stay."

I said, "Hal, Anchor might train off. Three-year-olds do this time of year. That's one reason why the Breeders' Cups are so valuable - separates the champs from the almost champs."

"But you're willing to take that chance with Feathers?"

"You know he's a two-year-old. And lightly raced."

"I'll pay all your personal expenses. I've spoken to the trainer who keeps my American-based runners, and he has agreed to stable the horse in Florida."

"And Feathers? If I decide he should stay here and run?"

"Yes, and Feathers. I've a paternalistic interest in that horse ever since I financed the trade for Lonelyheart. Come on, be a sport!"

Happy was nodding vehemently.

I caved in without any more pressure. "Sure. Thanks, Hal. 'Bye now." I replaced the receiver and hugged Happy.

As soon as I'd overseen the shipping of Feathers and Anchor to Hal's Hialeah trainer's yard near Miami, Happy and I left on a plane for Arkansas.

21

Racecourses, out of season, are very desolate places. Oaklawn, in Arkansas, was no exception. The lush green leaves, which in spring and summer hung heavy on its tall trees, now had turned to crimson, or to rust.

We entered its precinct where cement-jockey statues stood tall near the leaning rails in front of the main grandstand, there was no festive atmosphere. Happy and I had agreed to meet Whitey's former assistant trainer, Norman Hawk, there. Sour, disappointed and angry, he felt unfairly dismissed by the new trainer at the yard, and vented his fury as he spoke.

"Awful shit turned me out like I was a leper. Why? I'd been good for the yard, preparing your Lonelyheart to win next season's Derby here," Norman crushed out a lit cigarette as if he was stomping on the new trainer.

I countered, "The guy must have his reasons, I suppose."

"No! None! I'm one of the good guys. But let me tell you something, I think he knows a secret about Whitey's death, and he doesn't want to open that can of worms. He likes being top man at the yard, like training Lonelyheart, as a top contender for next year's Arkansas Derby."

"Secret?"

"Yup. Mind you, there could be one. Whitey kept one huge secret himself, that he was a Jew. Here in the Southland, it's not easy being a Jew. The Ku Klux Klan always had it in for them. Always hated them, just like the Arabs always hated them. So he changed his name, from Whiteman, he became Whitey."

"That's not much of a secret," Happy said, having just come from New York where there were thousands of name alterations. "My pal, the actress Sybil Sykes, told me her name was originally Silverstein."

"Okay, in Hollywood, and New York, maybe Miami, but not so easy in Arkansas. There's more, of course. It was rumored he'd switched Feathers."

"That's nonsense. I can swear to it. Look at Feathers' performance this season. One of the best two-year-olds in Britain, and also the US."

"News travels fast. Here in Arkansas we know all about his career in England. And at Belmont. Yup. Doesn't make a grain of difference. Story is that when he made the trade he had no idea how good Feathers would become."

"I don't believe it. From the moment he arrived in my yard when I tested his legs, looked in his eyes, and saw his action I knew he was special. Whitey surely knew that, too."

"So, why was he killed? Yup, I'm certain he didn't die a natural death from a heart attack. He was sound as a fiddle. Ate careful, drank little, and had just paid $1,000 to join a gym."

"Norman, that's what my wife and I are here to find out." I offered him a fresh cigarette. He was one heavy smoker. He'd gone through the last two in my pack.

"So let's go to the cemetery. I think if Whitey's exhumed, and there's an autopsy - which the new trainer in his yard refused to permit - we'll discover there was monkey business."

We went to the Jewish cemetery. Sad place. The evergreens weren't even green. There were no flowers, not allowed. The graves were barely marked with short plaques. Whitey's relatives had insisted he was buried under the name Whiteman.

Happy, her face wet with tears, asked the caretaker, "What would it take to get this man exhumed?"

"A court order, ma'am. And you'll need a damned good reason for a court order."

I went to see the local coroner. He listened to my suspicions. Whitey's body was exhumed, and it was discovered that he had died of cyanide poisoning.

That information didn't thrill his relatives. They were horrified, and insisted a case be opened to determine who could have been responsible for giving him cyanide. They insisted that Whitey would never have committed suicide, and certainly not by such a painful means.

Happy and I thought we knew the answer, but didn't offer it. There was too much more to be done in other states.

We flew to Florida to check on the well being of our two potential runners stabled there, but not before making a visit to Lonelyheart. He neighed with glee on seeing Happy. And he accepted a few pats from me.

22

Bono, a Roman Catholic, could not be cremated. His relations had insisted that his body be sent to them in California, where they planned to keep it in the morgue until all his cousins descended on Hollywood for the funeral.

Happy and I went straight to California to the morgue that was holding Bono's remains. I asked the morgue-keeper, "Any chance Bono Munoz was poisoned? Any trace of cyanide in his body?"

"How'd you know?" He eyed me suspiciously. He went to his telephone and dialed. I wondered if he was calling the police.

He wasn't. I heard him say into the mouthpiece, "Mr. Munoz, there's some character here nosing around and asking if cyanide was found in your cousin's body. What should I do with him? Restrain him here? Sure, if you want that."

Happy and I were kept at the morgue like unwillingly sequestered jurors on a difficult case.

The cousin showed up quickly. He looked like Bono, with frizzy oily hair, hooded eyes, and thick lips. He had a pronounced Mexican accent.

"Hola!" He slapped the morgue-keeper on the back with both hands as if they were longtime friends." These are the troublemakers?"

"Yeah. What's this about cyanide?"

"*Dios mio, cyanide! Era eso.* I knew there had been something not right in this. Born a Catholic, Bono never would take his own life. *Nunca*! So, what do you know? Why you have come here with this garbage about cyanide? You want to upset my mother, Bono's *tia*?"

I put on my most level expression. "I don't want to upset anybody. I used to be Bono's assistant trainer, and I've taken it upon myself to look into his death. Mainly, because two of the other trainers we had met at Arlington two years ago are now dead. Also cyanide poisoning."

Mr. Munoz wept like a child whose bicycle had been stolen, and crashed. "My poor auntie, she knew he wouldn't die so young of an *attaque de corazon*. No, not possible. Too healthy. Buy why poison him? That dear, lovely Bono hadn't an *enemigo* on this earth."

My own memories of 'dear, lovely Bono' didn't quite match. I said, "With your permission, as his closest of kin, will you allow the morgue to give us a certificate of death that lists cyanide as the cause?"

Munoz dried his eyes. "You'll have to pay for the certificate."

I pulled out my checkbook and obliged him.

Nile was still in the Munoz stable for the time being. I went to Nile where Bono had left him - at the stable near Belmont. He remembered me and neighed joyfully.

Seeing my four old friends in their horse boxes and finding them well and in prime condition, gladdened my heart.

With Munoz's death certificate in hand, Happy and I went to the coroner's office. It wasn't far from JFK Airport.

"You again?" He echoed the other Saratoga coroner of two years ago when I fingered the murderer of the three girl jockeys by blowing her cover.

"Yes." I slapped Bono Munoz's death certificate on his desk and said, "And we've been to Arkansas where we learned Whitey was poisoned with cyanide, too."

Happy, who'd spent the long flying hours musing on how and why my fellow trainers had died, now took a bottle of aspirin from her handbag.

"Have the pills from this bottle analyzed. I'm sure you'll find cyanide in them."

"Where did you get those pills? There's got to be a reason for analyzing them. That's an expensive procedure."

"There is," I assured him. "You see, these pills were given to my wife by another trainer, a Saudi, named Hassan Massoud. In fact, he gave her *two* such bottles; the first at the races in England, and another in Dubai. Thank God she didn't take any of the aspirin he gave her - or..." I almost fainted at the thought.

"I don't follow you."

"We've mulled over Hassan's purpose and we came to the conclusion that he wanted to murder both of us to get my owners. Which is the same reason why he killed Whitey, van der Holt, and Bono Munoz. To get their owners. He had so damn few."

"But why aspirin?"

"He makes them himself in Dubai. He has lots of businesses there and I discovered one is a jewelry firm that uses cyanide to extract gold and silver from ore, and another is a pharmaceutical manufacturing - over-the-counter stuff, like aspirin."

"Yeah, and?"

Happy completed the explanation. "He figured that people just put a bottle of aspirin in their medicine cabinet and use it when they get a headache. That was why Whitey died first, then van der Holt. They died when they had headaches and took the poisoned aspirin. Bono made it easier for Hassan, telling him in the limo he had a headache."

The coroner said nothing. He nodded, got up from his desk, and shook first Happy's hand, then mine.

We were ushered out of his ugly fluorescent-lit office as if we were royalty.

Hollywood royalty did meet us outside. Sybil had brought us to the coroner's office in her limousine. We toasted one another with champagne from the limo's bar, and headed back to the airport to go to Miami so I could get to work my two runners.

Sybil came with us. She bought two Florida-breds, and learned the bliss of an owner - watching your own horse flesh at the gallop.

By November 2nd, we were all three at Churchill Downs - home of the Kentucky Derby in early May. But this was November, and the crowds were thinner, less exuberant, and typically attended by more serious racegoers. I didn't hear a single 'rebel yell' out of the crowd. Sybil got more attention than the horses in the Breeders Cup parade. Racegoers' heads swiveled to catch a glimpse of her famous face, see what she was wearing and whom she was with.

Feathers won his race. Captain and Mrs. Ainsley were present, and now they had plenty of cash for trips, thanks to Feathers.

Arrow didn't win. But I'd always known, although he was a good horse, he wasn't a great horse. He'd win again next season, in minor races, and good kind Hal Murphy would be satisfied with that.

"Ah'm goin' t'send mah hawse t'England." Sybil said in the fake Kentucky accent she planned to use in the movie, 'but as them's Florida-bred hawses, we all should bring 'em back t'Hialeah t'run in Florida too." Happy and I hoped she'd ease up on the mountain talk in social situations; now *we* were embarrassed.

Using perfect elocution, Happy asked her, "Could we go to Kentucky for the yearling sales? That's where we'll find the best of the best." Loyal Kentucky-bred girl that she is, Happy wasn't going to let an opportunity to return home go by.

We celebrated with great sex that night.

Happy whispered, "Let's go back to Paw's farm for a visit. Sex there is always just like it was on our wedding night.

We did. I drove her over the hills and up into the mountains to take her home again.

About the Author

BEA CAYZER, daughter of a US Ambassador-at-Large, lived eighteen years in South America where her first husband's cousin owned the ten-time winner of the national steeplechase. With her second husband, Britisher Major Stanley Cayzer, a longtime Director of his family's shipping companies, they had racehorses winning all over England: IMPORT won the Wokingham at Royal Ascot, the Stewards' Cup at Goodwood, KING ALFRED bested The Queen's FIFE AND DRUM at Chepstow, and ADMIRAL'S BARGE beat top horseman Robert Sangster's champion at Haydock. Her literary output includes three non-fiction bestsellers. Her magazine articles appeared in *Town & Country, House & Garden, Esquire, Show, Harper's, Travel* and her own publication, *Palm Beach Tattler*. She has three daughters: Mary Holguin and Claudia Holguin, who live in Palm Beach, and Jeannie Roberts who lives with her British husband in France. Bea has just completed a new Happy Harrow mystery and has a third in the works. Her horse racing interest continues as she has a share in GAELIC DANCER, with bloodlines stretching to NORTHERN DANCER, NIJINSKY and NUREYEV on the sire's side and MR. PROSPECTOR and DANZIG on the dam's.

www.ingramcontent.com/pod-product-compliance
Lightning Source LLC
Chambersburg PA
CBHW031505270326
41930CB00006B/266